# Pieces of Mind

# *Pieces of Mind*

Fragmented Commentary
On Domestic Blisters and
Living Laughably Ever After

Marilyn Dittoe

The Wooster Book Company
Wooster • Ohio

The Wooster Book Company
205 West Liberty Street • Wooster Ohio • 44691



Printed in the United States of America.

**ISBN 1-888683-77-5**

*Library of Congress Cataloging-In-Publication Data*

Dittoe, Marilyn

Pieces of mind : fragmented commentary on domestic blisters and living laughably ever after / Marilyn Dittoe.

p. cm.

ISBN 1-888683-77-5 (pbk. : alk. paper)

1. Family life—Humor. I. Title.

PN6231.F3D58 1998

814'.54—dc21 98-30175

CIP

This book is printed on acid-free paper.

Author's Note: *I dedicate this work of questionable literary value to Betty Cocklin, my English teacher turned friend and mentor. You were as strict a taskmaster in the classroom as you are a fine role model in life. You have my undying gratitude for "sprinkling seeds on fertile ground," as you so humbly put it. Your influence is perennial.*

# Contents

*Profound Observations On Piddly Occurrences*

Quality Time—You Get What You Pay For 3
Reflux, Reduce, or Refinance, Then Reunite 6
Party Animal Tells All 9
Firm but Friendly—Just the Ticket 11
The Lowdown on Touchdowns and Goosedown 13
Garbage, I Mean, *Garage* Sale 16
Things That Go Bump in the Night 19

*Dysfunction—It's All Relative*

Not in My Job Description 25
Such a Deal 27
Mud Mothers on Pumpkin Perfection 29
Freezing Our Assets 31
Other Mother Pampers Campers 33
Sideline Psychosis—Sane at the Game 36
Tough Love Whimps Out 39

*All Critters Dear and Despicable*

Shedding Some Misconceptions About Man's Best Friend 45
Of Pigs and Prophets 48
Household Under Siege—De-tails Fuzzy 51
The Buzzwords: Make My Day 53
New Tricks? Who's Doing the Teaching? 55
Making a Mountain out of a Mouse Tale 58

*Annoyances—Fingernails On the Chalkboard of Life*

A Common Cooking Whine 63
Technical Support Services: Direct Line to the Divine 66

It's Over When the Out-of-Tone Lady Sings 69
Designs for Splashing Get Tongue Lashing 72
Dryer Does Double Duty as Slot Machine 74
Ching-Ching, It's Spring 77
Talking Trash About College Cash 79
I'm Dreaming of a Night Sniffless 81
Summer Travelers Over a Barrel 84
Mayday! Mayday! Mom in Distress! 87

*Theories and Epiphanies (And a Few Revelations From No Woman's Land)*

Just Say No 93
We Went and Spent to Vent 96
"Lifting" the Veil—Dangerous Business for Women 99
Real Van Can Wear Pink 101
Odiferous and Sensuous, Scents-R-Us 104
Serious About the Series 107
The Pursuit of Mediocrity 109

*Passages: Worry a Little, Whine a Little, Then Suck It Up and Move On*

An Easy Delivery (re: My First Column) 113
Braving the Birds and the Bees 115
Kissing Boo-Boos Pooh-Poohed as No-No for Mama 118
Animal, Vegetable, Mineral, or Chemical? A Hairy Decision 121
Mall-Adjusted Children 124
Campus Scenery: Babes vs. Plaster Cows 126
Graduation Traumatization 129
Mom's First Prom 131

# *Pieces of Mind*

*Profound Observations*
*On Piddly Occurrences*

## *Quality Time—You Get What You Pay For*

SUNDAY WE HAD A FAMILY OUTING. Family outings used to mean going to the park or a zoo or museum. That was back when the kids were little and my husband and I had some control over our universe. Now we're operating under the chaos theory.

There's a sense of blackmail about the whole quality time issue. We have to bribe the kids to spend time with us.

You guessed it. Our family fun day landed us at the mall. When the kids proposed the idea, my husband got the old shoot-me-now look on his face. He'd opt for an appendectomy without anesthesia performed by a Japanese Steakhouse chef over shopping any day. But I shamed him into it with the "Family Time Together" argument.

So we went. And of course we wound up spending all our time at clothing stores with names which I will, because of my journalistic integrity, change to The Chasm, Old Branch of the Military, American Tufted Titmouse, and Eddie Crew.

My husband just doesn't understand kids' need to buy clothing. I've tried to explain it to him. It's really quite simple. Kids grow at a rate that is approximately triple the rate of inflation, so that in a formula where X = inflation, 3X = Y + Q squared to the !#$% power. This means, for you non-quantitative types, that a year ago you could buy an entire pubescent ensemble including a T-shirt with the flavor of the month rock band design, boxer shorts suitable for viewing above the belt line, and pants of astounding largeness, for the same amount of money that you will this year spend on a single metal alloy toe ring. It also means that when you have to replace the outfit because your kid is beginning to grow into the pants, you'll have to head over to Harry's Big and Tall Shop to get some that are proportionally larger than the actual size 29 he wears in geek size.

But I'm getting off the track. As I was saying, for some reason my husband has difficulty grasping the whole process of teen wardrobe replenishment. He has this absurd idea that it's an unnecessary expenditure of money.

This could be because the word "fashion" for him has about the same meaning as the word "quark" has for the rest of us. (Look it up.) He actually still has clothing in his closet from high school and, much to my dismay, still occasionally places some of it upon his person. I've tried to talk him into getting therapy for this.

When he heard our son saying he'd outgrown all his shorts, Dad offered him some of his. The boy went pale as I tried to explain to my husband that while short, tight polyester running shorts coupled with over-the-calf, striped tube socks is a good look for him, our son needs his own fashion identity. The kid owes me.

Anyway, as the kids and I browsed through Old Branch of the Military, I noticed Jim hyperventilating in a corner and suggested he walk it off by doing laps around the peripheral aisles and trying not to make eye contact with any price tags. A fish out of water, spasmodically twitching and flopping on a dry surface, would've looked comfortable by comparison. I'd swear when I came close to him I heard adding machine noises emanating from his head.

As we approached the checkout line, I whispered instructions to my younger daughter to distract Dad for a few minutes, distraction being her specialty. So she engaged him in an animated, albeit one-sided discussion, since his pupils were dilated and he was entering a mild stage of shock. We were then able to quickly pay for the clothes and pull him through the exit into the cold, crisp air of the parking lot.

"Did you enjoy the movie?" we asked him as his head cleared, hiding the bags behind our backs.

We're talking about the destruction of brain cells here. I don't care how the kids threaten me, next time we're going to the zoo.

## *Reflux, Reduce, or Refinance, Then Reunite*

NOTHING STRIKES FEAR INTO THE HEART of a middle-aged woman like an upcoming high school reunion. It's sort of an involuntary muscle response—like when you sneeze you always have to close your eyes. When a woman finds out the date of her class reunion, inevitably her very next thought is her hip measurement and whether she'll have enough time to decrease it.

Don't ask me why this is. I don't know autonomic reflex from gastric reflux. I just know I do a lot of both in the weeks leading up to a class reunion.

A friend of mine recently went to her thirtieth year high school reunion. I will hereafter refer to her as Pamm, with two "m's", in the interest of protecting her anonymity. (That should throw them off, Pam.) Anyway, she had fully intended, as so many of us do, to lose weight before her reunion, but just kept putting it off until the morning of the actual event. At that time, she reached the very reasonable conclusion that a fifteen pound weight loss over a six hour time period was a rather unrealistic goal, even for the very highly motivated. So she made the only sound decision any of us would have made under the circumstances. She went to an obscenely expensive dress shop she would never have considered going to unless she were really desperate, which she was, and bought an obscenely expensive, but remarkably slenderizing, black dress for that night. (Which, by the way, confirms my suspicion that movie stars and other really rich people aren't actually thinner than the rest of us—they can just afford clothes that make them look that way.)

So that night Pamm looked and felt like a million bucks. And I'm sure she'll bask in the afterglow of the many compliments she received until the end of the month, when the bill comes and her car and husband turn into a pumpkin and a white rat. But I'm sure she'll say it was well worth it, especially since she has ten years for economic recovery before her next reunion.

So what exactly is it about an impending class reunion that turns a sensible, self-possessed woman into a neurotic ninny? (Of course I'm not talking about you, Pamm.) Why would a little trek down memory lane toward high school and "the best years of our lives" make us examine ourselves in our underwear in front of a full-length mirror and inspect the skin under our eyes with microscopic intensity?

After all, a class reunion is not a cattle drive. It's not like they're going to route us all onto a stage where we'll be required to do quarter turns in front of a panel of judges consisting of the former captains of all the boys' varsity teams. They won't then hand us stick-on name tags that say, "Hello. My name is Marilyn." and either "I'm Dog Meat." or "I'm a Prime Cut." We're not going to have to prance around in swimsuits and high heels.

Let's not be absurd. Everyone there will be the same number of years past eighteen as we are. Everyone there will be sensitive about the subtle changes that mark the passage of time on our faces and figures. Come on, these are our old school chums—they'll be just as kind and non-judgmental about our flaws as they were back in high school. ...

Oh geez. We're hosed.

I can hear it now:

"Hey, Ralph. Did you see Marilyn? I'd say that babe's gettin' a little long in the tooth. Talk about going to seed. She'd be lucky if she could wear her old cheerleading skirt as a garter. Har-Har. Ho-Ho. etc."

They'll be having a knee-slapping good time, and I'll be across the room just waving away at them unsuspectingly with my chicken-flab arm jiggling to beat the band.

Heaven help me, I've got to do something fast. It's four weeks 'til my reunion. That's a pound a day by my calculations. I'd better get directions to that dress shop just in case.

## *Party Animal Tells All*

I'M BEGINNING TO DEVELOP A COMPLEX. Everywhere I go, under all types of circumstances, people I talk to manage to insert somewhere into the conversation, "You're not going to write about this, are you?"

People, people, people. Calm down. This is not *The Enquirer*. I wouldn't dream of cheapening my interpersonal relationships by airing intimate details for personal gain.

Except today.

(Sorry, S.P., it's just too good, and you dropped it right in my lap, girl. I think it was the headdress.)

The other night, the hubby and I attended a dinner/dance to benefit a local not-for-profit organization. You know, one of those baked rubber chicken over rice, stuffed shirt, sway a little and call it dancing affairs?

Wrong again, Mr. Vanderbilt.

This was a rip-roaring good party with great food for a wonderful cause—a win-win situation. Pure fun in good conscience. Plus, it was an irresistible opportunity to see many of the local "pillars" let down their hair, kick up their heels, and step light years out of their sophisticated public personas. This, my compadre, was a target-rich environment for the likes of your humble, local humor columnist.

So when this friend, whose name I will not mention but whose initials—in case you didn't catch them the first time—are S.P., stepped up to me, struck a defiant pose, and in no uncertain terms admonished me not to write about "this", I took one look at her uniquely-fashioned head gear and mask and thought, "Where's my pen?"

When someone hands it to you on a platter, perfectly garnished and ripe for the taking, whaddya gonna do? You swallow it whole, Bucko. That kind of self-denial just isn't good for you.

So here they all were, folks who sit in boardrooms, treat patients, and teach classes during the week, doing the Macarena and Electric Slide with reckless abandon, jerking and jiggling like Monday would never come. Then there was the snake dance that turned into more of a crack-the-whip before it was over. These people could cut a rug with the best of the Dick Clarkians, and don't you doubt it.

But I think the highlight of the evening, for me, was when someone delivered to our table a very large, pickled fish head. It had been spirited away from the buffet table, bedecked with a feathered party mask and grapes for eyes, and sported a large, fake gold coin in its pouting mouth. Who says grown-ups can't have fun? This was indeed a fitting jewel in the crown of a delightfully festive event.

What's funny to contemplate is how our kids envisioned our evening. No doubt it was something closer to the rubber chicken, stuffed shirt version of an adult good time. Little do they know how well the cat can play when the mice are away.

And of course, I told them it was quite a dignified occasion, and all behaved accordingly. Hey, turn about's fair play.

That's my story, and I'm sticking to it.

## *Firm but Friendly—Just the Ticket*

LAST WEEKEND PRODUCED A NEW ENTRY for the baby book. My daughter got her first speeding ticket. Granted, it wasn't as joyous an occasion as the first tooth, but it was a landmark. And I do believe it was nearly as painful for her as cutting teeth. Gnawing on a frozen teething ring wouldn't have offered much relief, however. She was too busy eating humble pie.

Before you jump to the collision, I mean *conclusion*, that I'm being insensitive to my daughter's feelings by writing about her mishap, let me just tell you that she's the one who suggested I write about it. She discovered, BY TELLING HALF OF WOOSTER ABOUT IT BEFORE SHE TOLD HER MOTHER AND FATHER, that sympathies tend to run a bit left-of-center, on the side of the child, in cases such as this one. This is especially true if the child in question has half the population believing her parents have a secret torture chamber in their basement wherein they stretch all offspring guilty of crimes against authority or traffic violations on a rack and shove bamboo shoots under their fingernails. I guess she thinks if the child welfare department throws us in lock-up, we'll be more likely to show her leniency.

How very cunning are the workings of the adolescent mind.

It's not that I think her endearingly emotional response to getting a ticket was insincere—I know she was genuinely upset. Imagine how the poor unsuspecting patrolman felt after he pulled her over and approached the driver's side window.

Considering how fast she was going, he must have expected some smart-mouthed hard case behind the wheel. He probably thought he'd need a bullet-proof vest, not a hankie. How's a tough, hard-nosed enforcer of law and order supposed to deal with a big-eyed, quivering blob of teenaged girl?

As it turns out, pretty darn well. He must have found exactly the right mark on the scale from tar-and-feathering to tender fathering, because he made quite an impression on the quivering blob. He made her see the error of her ways *and* think he was a really nice person at the same time. According to what she told us, this guy could be the expert on child discipline for the new millennium. Officer Spock.

Maybe once he got a gander at Pink Floyd, our uniquely appointed minivan, he was forewarned that a sympathetic approach was in order. One wouldn't, after all, expect the operator of such a piece of vehicular fluff to carry an automatic weapon.

Further, after seeing my daughter's last name, he recognized that Floyd was the van of literary legend and requested that if this incident end up in the newspaper, he be referred to as "Officer Doe." He even scrawled his name illegibly on the ticket so I'd have no choice but to honor his request.

It's heartwarming to know Wooster's finest are humble as well as heroic.

Why heroic? Because in gently scaring my daughter out of her wits, he may very well have saved her life. I could've told her to slow down from now until she qualified for the Indy 500 or melted the tires down to their rims, whichever came first. But what he told her had far more impact (eek—*scary word*).

So Officer Doe—wherever you are—thank you. And if it's not too much trouble, would you mind stopping by and telling her to clean her room?

## *The Lowdown on Touchdowns and Goose Down*

FREEZER BURN CAN BE A REAL ANNOYANCE, especially when it's on your toes. Anyone who was at the last high school football game knows whereof I speak. Don't try to deny it. Half of you folks were huddled with me in the women's restroom third quarter trying to thaw out.

And as if that weren't enough toe abuse, the next day I refroze them, a procedure much frowned upon by the USDA, at the Ohio State game in Columbus.

But I have to say, from the ankles up I was nice and toasty. That's because of this wonderful garment I have that some of my friends refer to as my Nanook of the North coat. Hey, I may not look like a page out of J. Crew, but when I leave a game to go home, my tooshie's fully ambulatory. You guys waddle like you left your behinds behind on the metal bleachers.

I picked this coat up on sale (no comments from the peanut gallery) several years ago and have taken no end of ribbing about it. When I wear it, I bear a strong resemblance to the Michelin Man, and it does take up a lot of space on the bleachers, but, by golly, when people see me coming they get out of my way. I cut a swath five feet wide when I move through a crowd. Bodies fly. If I were on the field, the quarterback could hand the ball off to me and I'd for sure break right through that line.

So anyway, my family, some friends, my Nanook coat and I braved the deep freeze and went to the OSU vs. Minnesota game. You could tell the Minnesota fans from us Buckeyes because we looked like rolled sausages in our layers, and the Minnesota fans just looked amused. Before I knew it, our little group had joined the surging throng of humanity under the stadium. We were heat-seeking missiles in search of hot chocolate, and of course, all the concession stands had run out. Ultimately, we settled for a very expensive cup of undrinkable coffee and took turns warming our hands over it.

You might assume the reason I'd subject myself and my loved ones to this hardship would be, purely and simply, love of the game of football. To this, I would reply by chortling with unbridled amusement at having given you such an impression. Well okay, I do love watching the high school games, but I go to the OSU games for completely different reasons. It's the circus atmosphere that draws me there: Block "O", the band, the cheerleaders, the stadium crazies. You have to understand, my knowledge of the game is rudimentary at best, and my familiarity with its finer points is comparable to my comprehension of nuclear fusion.

All I know is that two lines of very large-necked guys repeatedly slam into each other in a kind of choreographed mosh dance in an effort to move the ball down the mosh pit and score (or prevent the other dance line from doing so). Aside from that, there are all kinds of unappreciated aggression like mask-grabbing, hitting each other with clippers, and interfering in situations that evidently don't concern you resulting in such punitive actions as flag-flinging and losing your down, which is really bad in this cold weather. There are even some procedures that are downright illegal and, presumably, could result in lawsuit.

It's all so complicated that what I do is watch Block "O" and when they start fluttering their cards excitedly, I know there's something important happening on the field. Then, when the cheerleaders do the fight song pompom routine, I know we've either scored or made some other significant advance in the game. Next, I check the scoreboard for confirmation. It's and unbeatable system.

But the one remaining thing I don't understand is why the players bother with all those pads and safety gear. All they'd really need would be Nanook coats and they'd be invincible.

## *Garbage, I Mean,* Garage *Sale*

WHOEVER SAID "THE BEST THINGS IN LIFE ARE FREE" apparently missed my garage sale. Well, it wasn't exactly mine, but my daughter's ... that is, she's the one who made the money.

It all started the day I went on what turned into an archeological dig in my basement. I was trying to locate an old set of encyclopedias (just in case anyone needed outdated information) and in the process found artifacts that would require carbon dating for identification purposes. I would swear I also saw Mayan ruins down there. And me without a machete.

Anyway, I returned hours later, gasping for air and covered with cobwebs. But for the grace of God and the trail of crumbs from the donut I was eating on the way down, I would never have found my way out. But just like they say in Reader's Digest, sometimes a life-threatening experience can help a person become more centered, more in touch with her feelings and priorities. It did that for me. I knew what I had to do. And if my husband hadn't wrestled me to the ground and wrenched the matches from my trembling fingers, I would have torched the basement.

He suggested as an alternative a garage sale, to which I replied, "YOU CAN'T MAKE ME GO BACK IN THERE."

At this point, my fourteen year old daughter, alias "She of Entrepreneurial Spirit," said she would be glad to do it for me for a mere pittance—the proceeds from the sale. And as I looked deep into her eyes, noting in passing the irises had assumed the shape of dollar signs just like in cartoons, I thought, yes, this woman-child is ready for the garage sale rite of passage. She will meet the challenge and prevail. And I turned and ran for my life up the stairs, shamelessly leaving her alone in that subterranean jungle.

The next thing I knew, she was throwing a party. Far be it from her to miss a social opportunity. With the boom box blaring, she and a couple friends relentlessly dusted, sorted, priced, and pitched their way through the ruins. These kids today are made of some pretty stern stuff.

When I finally worked up the courage to go down and check on their progress, I found them playing with an impressive collection of My Little Ponies, wearing some rather eclectic, retro get-up, and taking pictures of each other with a Polaroid camera. One has to allow for a little regression at major developmental stages. After all, I sucked my thumb for an hour after the encyclopedia quest.

Then the big day arrived. The ad had run, the signs were up, and it was time to open the garage door to the surging masses of humanity that waited outside. All one of her. She did buy some things, though, and as word spread far and wide of the unique treasures offered at bargain prices, that slow drip of customers turned into what would almost qualify as an occasional drip. But this was probably a good thing because we were experiencing a certain amount of seller's remorse. Little by little, the merchandise was mysteriously finding its way back into the house. My daughter, of course, found this disappearing act quite distressing as it could have had a direct effect on her profits and mean she had had that party in the basement for nothing.

So we devised a system for legitimately determining what could be withdrawn from the sale. We called it the lump-in-the-throat factor. Anything that evoked a true emotional response was allowed reentry into the house. For my husband, it was a stupid little pewter plate with a bent rim and a hunt print etched in the center. Mind you, I'm not saying his emotions weren't genuine—I'm too sensitive to say that—I'm just saying he was being a real Bozo. My choice was something with far more sentimental value: the kids' potty seat. And for some other people in the family, and I won't mention any names because they are getting old enough that for it to become publicly known would bring shame, ridicule, and social ostracism, there were a few stuffed animals.

Ultimately, things worked out pretty well. My daughter made a decent chunk of change to compensate for all the partying she had to do, and I'm not nearly as terrified to go down to the basement as I once was. The problem is, she didn't sell even half the stuff, and I won't let her bring it back into the house. She's planning another sale soon. In the meantime, I'm terrified to go into the garage.

## *Things That Go Bump in the Night*

About 2:00 this morning my husband and I were jolted awake by the long, grating creak of a door being opened.

My husband was, I think, a bit disoriented. He jumped out of bed saying something about a hummingbird, threw on his robe and some running shoes, and charged outside. I guess he was just trying to uphold his duty as the great protector, in light of all the senseless violence wreaked by bands of marauding hummingbirds in our area recently. After all, a man's gotta do what a man's gotta do.

Meantime, I was left to face the demons within. And this I did by waking up my dog, who is seventy-seven in people years, and sending him out of the bedroom into the great, dark unknown of the house to do what a dog's gotta do. He made it about five feet into that great unknown before lowering himself stiffly into his favorite position and resuming his nap.

You just can't get good help anymore.

So it was left to me to find the source of the sinister creak, and since I'd watched *The X Files* right before bed, I wasn't operating from a false feeling of security. My senses were keenly focused and my reflexes sharp as I bravely held onto my bedroom door jamb and stretched to flip on the living room light. I knew I could be dealing with any of a number of dangers including, but not limited to, scaly one-eyed creatures with dripping fangs, mutant multi-headed killer goats, or even zombie aliens arisen from a chemical dump site. I had no delusions. So when I lost my grip and fell forward onto the living room carpet, my nightgown flipping up over my head, I was less than patient with Jim's chuckling reaction. He'd returned home from the Great Hummingbird Wars showing little evidence that the cold night air had cleared his head.

We decided to divide and conquer. Jim went downstairs to check for basement invaders and I headed upstairs in search of encroachers parachuting in from enemy helicopters. It seemed like a fair deal to me.

It occurred to me halfway up the stairs that I should've grabbed a kitchen knife or my pepper spray and that Jim, too, was unarmed as we don't keep a baseball bat by our bedroom door like they always do in the movies. For that matter, the only pieces of athletic equipment in our room are my exercise machine and a few golf tees on the dresser. Well, I thought, if we catch the fiend we can always drag him back to our room and make him do twenty minutes on the Healthrider while we poke him in the eyes with golf tees.

We found nothing. Nada. Zilch. The kids were snug and snoring, the cat was outside, the guinea pig—who can't open doors anyway—was asleep, and the aforementioned dog was practically comatose.

Jim was back to sleep in 30 seconds flat, presumably dreaming of performing remarkable feats of valor defending democracy against the threat of aviary attack around the globe. But not me. Oh no. I lay there, frozen in place, listening to every little creak, pop, and shift of the house and flinching with each one.

It's infuriating how black and white everything is to men. We heard a noise, we searched the house, we found nothing, and he satisfied himself with some silly explanation about the wind causing it and went right back to sleep. Right. The highest winds we've ever experienced *inside* our house occurred the last time I made chili, and what we heard then sure wasn't the creaking of doors. His explanation just didn't wash with me.

So I did guard duty for the rest of the night, certain that at any moment an ax-wielding maniac would crash into our room demanding money and jewels in exchange for our lives.

Okay, so I'm a little tired today and he's perking away like the energizer bunny. *Somebody* had to be responsible for our family's welfare. And I plan to be ready for action again tonight. Nobody'll mess with my house and my family while I have anything to say about it.

But for now I think I'll just curl up on the rug next to the dog and grab a little shut-eye. Wake me up at bedtime.

## *Dysfunction —*
## *It's All Relative*

## *Not in My Job Description*

In the '90s, division of household duties is a tricky thing. We may not be beating the laundry against rocks in the river anymore (possibly because the river is far dirtier than the clothes) or carving new spokes for the wagon wheels, but there's still a lot to do.

The sensible thing is for the most qualified person to do it... or at least make it look that way. That's the tricky part, and it occasionally runs cross-grain with feminist philosophy. I, for example, don't cut the grass. I'm frightfully certain that big, mean lawn tractor is just too complicated and powerful for the likes of little ol' me. Besides, I used to have to do it all the time when I was a kid, and the Scarlett O'Hara thing's been working like a dream on my husband. Gloria Steinem may disapprove, but she can just go sweat buckets and develop liver spots on her own lawn. I have no conscience about such things. I don't suppose there's much call for lawn mowing out there on the speaking circuit anyway.

Don't get me wrong. I have a lot of regard for Ms. Steinem's new and improved philosophy. I heard her speak a few years ago, and I understand that the message is, roughly, that women should seize the day and feel good about their choices and accomplishments, whatever they may be. So in light of that, I think Gloria would be proud of me when I say I feel really good about making the choice not to mow the lawn and through evasion and manipulation have managed to avoid doing it for nearly two decades of married life. I can seize the day with the most dogged of feminists. In fact, I've been having these seizures once a week every summer for twenty years, and I plan to continue seizing for many years to come—or at least until we hit the lottery and have someone named Giles to mow the lawn.

My husband, in turn, never defrosts the freezer. He claims his choice not to do so falls somewhere under the heading of traditional family values. It must be in very fine print. His reasoning puzzles me somewhat, but I figure as long as I don't have to mow the lawn, why tamper with the delicate balance of power in our relationship? Marriage is a marvelous and mystical thing. Oh, sweet mystery of life … and lawns and freezers.

The kids have developed a very sophisticated technique of their own for, shall we say, delegating. They sit on their hineys until I do it for them. They know a mom's nervous system can only tolerate so many passes through a room without removing an abandoned, half-filled glass of milk sitting within striking range of a cat. They know they can always wait me out. They know the threat of an eternally stinky carpet far outweighs any half-blown ideas I may have about teaching them to be responsible human beings. And this knowledge empowers them. They seize the moment and no doubt feel good about their choice. What incredibly enlightened children I'm raising!

So as you can see, at our home we've all clearly identified what we aren't willing to do: Me, mow the lawn; Jim, defrost the freezer; and the kids, much of anything unless I threaten to do my high school pompom routine the next time they have friends over. But even though it probably sounds like our household runs like a well-oiled machine, there is still one area of difficulty.

We're all hoping for a visit from the litter box fairy—or maybe Gloria Steinem.

## *Such a Deal*

BUT, MOM, THEY ONLY COST SIX DOLLARS, and all you have to do is shorten them a little."

My son came home from a recent shopping trip with a pair of pants big enough to accommodate Yokozuna. When he puts them on, the waistband drops down and hangs precariously on his hip bones, and he looks like he has webbed legs. Even if I cross my eyes and stand on my head, I can't appreciate the look.

For one thing, my social conscience tells me it's a shameful waste of resources. There's more fabric in those pants than in the mooring cover of an average-sized ski boat. I mean, there are people right here in our very community who are forced to wear pants that only one person can fit into. It's enough to break your heart.

What's more, these new mega pants don't even cover the essential areas. If it weren't for the fashionable underlayers the kids wear, they'd look like a generation of refrigerator repairmen. My sources tell me that there are even a bold few who wear them *below* the actual gluteal region. I saw a group of kids with a boombox the other day and for an instant thought they were reenacting the penguin dance scene from *Mary Poppins*.

But back to my son's droopy drawer dilemma. In all fairness, I have to admit he doesn't routinely wear pants that are so much at odds with gravity. I think their purchase was more an economic decision than a fashion one. Nonetheless, damage control measures must be pursued.

I suppose I could put him on growth hormones and suggest he accessorize with an ax and an ox named Babe. Or maybe I'll just have to give in and alter the darn things, though admittedly I've never been a wizard with needle and thread. Taking up the pants legs won't be a problem, but transferring the crotch from the vicinity of the knees northward a foot or so to its natural habitat will present a real challenge. Nothing my high school Home Ec teacher taught me could've prepared me for this. It's a quantum leap from tea towels to the surgical technique required for total crotch replacement.

This is all my husband's fault, you know. He's got these convoluted money-saving ideas that usually result in my trying to figure out what to do with some great bargain he picked up somewhere. His best line of defense is always, "If nothing else, we can always put geraniums in it and put it on the front porch." I'm telling you, if I didn't work feverishly to keep these economical impulses of his at bay, our front yard would look like the city dump in a riot of crimson bloom, sort of like Andy Warhol in Monet's garden.

And like father, like son.

Now that I think about it, this isn't E.F. Hutton Jr.'s first fling with frugality. He bought a couch at Goodwill for two dollars once. Of course, there was no way to get it home and no place to put it once it was here, not to mention it's questionable origins, but true bargain-hunting genius can't be dissuaded by practicalities.

I guess I'd better get busy and work some tailoring magic on these pants. If I really botch things up, I could just blast them with some heavy-duty starch until they stand on their own. They'd make a pretty novel way to display geraniums, don't you think? And cheap, too.

## *Mud Mothers On Pumpkin Perfection*

THE OTHER DAY, WE WENT with some friends of ours to the pumpkin farm. It was rainy and freezing cold, but the kids wouldn't let us off the hook. They said it was tradition. They said it wouldn't be October without it. They said they really, really, really wanted to go. They implied they'd make our lives miserable if we didn't comply with their request. We know how good they are at that. We gave in.

On the way there, we adults made the best of the situation by offering an expansive travelogue about the breathtaking scenery. We said fascinating things like, "Look kids, doesn't that hillside look like a pallet of burnished bronzes, coppers, and golds?" And the kids responded with extensive eye-rolling and impatient questions about how long it would take to get there.

But once we arrived, their enthusiasm kicked in along with the thrill of acquisition as they tripped gaily among the vines in search of the perfect pumpkin.

We moms stood ankle-deep in freezing cold mud shouting encouragement and just generally being good, supportive parents while the dads sat in the warm car listening to a football game. That's okay, I thought. While he's in there staying warm, I'm out here racking up the brownie points so when we get old, they'll put him in a home and ask me to move in with them. That way, I can continue supplying them with invaluable advice while Mr. Armchair Quarterback's making potholders in an activity room somewhere.

But after about fifteen minutes with my toes marinating in the glacial ooze, the rain beating down on my head, and my fingers turning into popsicles, my maternal nurture began to wane. Soon my friend and I were using stronger language to motivate the kids.

"If you kids don't pick out your pumpkins NOW and get into the car, we're going to drive off and leave you, and you'll have to walk back to town carrying your ever-loving pumpkins. DO YOU HEAR ME?"

So they grudgingly made their choices and piled into the car, transforming it into what looked like a rolling mud wrestling-pit.

Then, just as we were pulling away, the dreaded words came from the other mom's youngest: "Mom, I didn't find one I liked. Can we look in the next field?"

Before we could slide a protest between our chattering teeth, she said, "Look—over there—I see one!" and jumped out and ran into a fresh, new, unexplored pumpkin patch toward the gourd of her dreams. By then, they'd all started looking alike to me; orange, leering, and malevolent. But when she held up her prize for her mother's approval, my survival instinct took over.

I beseeched my friend, "For the love of all that's precious and pure, woman, tell her you love that pumpkin more than life itself."

She did. And convincingly, too, for a woman whose face was frozen and whose improvisational ability was, thus, severely impaired. At that moment, I was proud to belong to the sisterhood of motherhood, and prouder yet to be her friend.

I'm thawed out now and looking back at our sojourn into pumpkin Hades in a more favorable light, selectively remembering only the good as a woman does after childbirth. I have to. How else could I face the prospect of December and picking out a Christmas tree?

## *Freezing Our Assets*

THOUGH IT MAY BE IMPOSSIBLE for some of you to believe, my husband and I have a slight difference of opinion on something. I think the thermostat should be set at seventy degrees, and he seems to feel that if a thin layer of ice forms in the toilet bowls, it's a simple enough matter to break it with a sharp tap of the bowl brush.

If you're planning to stop over for a visit, enter at your own risk. A good rule of thumb is, if you've been training for the Iditarod you should be okay. Otherwise you may want to invest in a hermetically-sealed suit. I hope this doesn't discourage you. We love company. The higher the body count, the more heat generated.

Once again, economy is at the heart of the issue. In my husband's mind, if we just chill a little now, in a few years we can more comfortably send the kids to college. He may be right. And with the numerous and diverse scholarship monies available, maybe we can benefit from one offered to victims of hypothermia.

That's not, however, much consolation to the kids and me. Walk into our living room on any given winter night and what you'll see is our couch with at least one chrysalis attached to it. That would be one of the kids or me wrapped in a comforter waiting for spring. Chances are the rest of us have fled to the warmth of a friend's house, the library, or even the grocery store for relief. But, ching-ching, just imagine the money we're saving. Cold cash.

Even Jim has to admit there is a down side to all this. No, brushing his teeth while wearing down-filled mittens doesn't bother him. Even having his tongue stick to his fork at dinnertime doesn't weaken his resolve. But sleeping with a woman who has more layers than the earth's crust seems to be trying his patience. Believe me, Victoria's Secret is nowhere near as well hidden as mine. And to top it off, my fingers are like popsicles.

But, hey, he's the man with the plan.

Speaking of secrets, I'll let you in on a little one: The kids and I have been scamming ol' Dad this year. As soon as he's out the door to work, we beeline to the thermostat and crank that baby up. Then before he comes home, we turn it back down to arctic air range. When he comes in at night, we all act natural as if we've been freezing away like dutiful little Eskimos all day. There's nothing like feeling like you're getting away with something to warm your extremities.

But lately I think he's getting a little suspicious. Perhaps it's because our movements aren't quite as stiff as they should be or because the icicles on the faucets are smaller than usual, but I think he's onto us. He's been barging in the door like he's trying to catch us in the act. He looks at us accusingly, feels the dog's nose, then checks the thermostat. Next, I suppose he'll start dusting it for prints. I'm afraid it's only a matter of time before he figures out our little scheme. Then I guess I'll have to come up with a more devious plan, one that will finally make him see reason.

Maybe I'll try wearing a snowsuit to bed.

## *Other Mother Pampers Campers*

I'VE SENT THREE KIDS to a total of ten summer sports camps over the past seven years. I think those are some pretty impressive statistics for a woman who abhors perspiration.

But that's what parenting is all about, isn't it? Making sacrifices for the good of our children even if it involves such horrors as digging sweaty soccer socks out of the bottom of a gym bag where they've been marinating for a week.

It's all worth it, though, when we see what marvelous benefits our children reap from the camp experience.

Aside from sharpening their athletic skills, one of the most important things they learn is self-sufficiency. That is, unless you have the dubious fortune of having an excellent sports camp right in your hometown. That's when camp isn't camp so much as it is a satellite residential experience with 24 hour, mom-on-call service.

This was the situation we had last week. I admit it, I thought maybe with the kiddo at camp ol' Mom might get to kick back a little. So when I dropped her, half her worldly possessions, and a year's supply of blow-pops—energy snack of champions—off at the dormitory, and said, "Call me if you need anything," I probably wasn't being totally sincere.

Big mistake. By the time I'd made the 10 minute trip home, I had a message on the answering machine to bring her a bag of ice. Apparently one of the girls had a cooler and they wanted to "chill their water" before their field session.

Now, I could be wrong, but I always thought of camp as a kind of "roughing it" experience, and ice struck me as sort of a luxury item. I saw no reason why they couldn't drink their water at field temperature. It would still be wet. So I stalled a little. And the call came again.

"Mom, *please* bring us some ice. So-and-so's mom is bringing bottles of spring water for us to put in the cooler."

Uh-oh. Peer pressure. And since there's nothing worse than being out-mommed, I took the ice.

A little later a call came for chapstick. I hesitated but was casually informed that so-and-so's mom was baking brownies to bring to camp.

At this point, I was beginning to become a little annoyed with so-and-so's mom's tendency toward over-achievement. Then I visualized the child of my womb attempting to eat a brownie through cracked and bleeding lips. I ran in with the chapstick.

Sometime later a call came for shower shoes—a bona fide request—and something, shamefully, I had forgotten to pack. Every mom who's ever sent a child to camp knows that standing in an institutional shower without shower shoes is tantamount to standing in a puddle of toxic waste. You can just kiss the healthy soles of your kid's feet goodbye if you forget shower shoes. What a pitiful excuse for a mother I was.

Meanwhile, so-and-so's mom was probably over there, making their beds, straightening their room, and vacuuming.

So I peeled out of the driveway and ignored all posted speed limits to get those rubber thongs to my beloved.

It's a good thing I didn't get pulled over.

"But officer, my child could be contracting athlete's foot and plantar's warts even as we speak!"

"You mean you sent her to camp without shower shoes?! Step out of the vehicle, put your hands on the roof of the car, and spread 'em!" he'd say with disdain. "And you call yourself a *mother*. You're a menace to society!"

The way things were going, so-and-so's mom would probably drive by and bail me out with a plate of homemade snickerdoodles.

By the time camp was over, I was thoroughly exhausted from the effort of meeting all of my daughter's slightest whims and was glad to get her home so I could relax a little. Then I remembered the mountain of putrid camp clothes in her gym bag.

For a while, I entertained the notion of calling so-and-so's mom to see if she'd come over and do the laundry for me. I'm so ashamed.

## *Sideline Psychosis—Sane at the Game*

I HAD AN OUT-OF-BODY EXPERIENCE last Sunday at my daughter's soccer game. Actually, that may be overstating it a bit. It was more like taking a step back and observing myself and the other parents as we cheered on the team.

It wasn't pretty. There we all were—teeth bared, eyes wild, veins bulging in our temples—keeping it all in perspective as we screamed like banshees.

I remember singing sweet bedtime lullabies to my child and sprinkling her little behind with baby powder, and I'm assuming my fellow screamers have similar memories. But we weren't sitting at this game yelling things like, "PLAY NICE—DON'T HIT—BE POLITE!" What was coming out of our mouths was primitive and unchecked. What a leap from the bassinet to the soccer field, from Wee Willy Winkie to "FIGHT FOR IT—KNOCK HER DOWN—GET THE BALL—NO MERCY!"

I think when we parents attend our kids' sporting events, we revert back to our origins in the caves. It's as if we're exhorting them to fight for that last hunk of meat from the carcass of a woolly mammoth.

Do you suppose the kids are confused by our altered attitudes? Based on my observations, my response would be a carefully considered "Heck, no!" They've got this latent cave thing lurking inside them, too. Just watch them. The minute they step onto the field, if you look closely, you can see their arms lengthen almost imperceptibly, their features coarsen, and their knuckles sprout more hair.

I don't want to contaminate perfectly good jock talk with literary allusions, but I can see a Jekyll and Hyde parallel here with perhaps a touch of *Lord of the Flies*. In fact, if William Golding were in the bleachers, I have no doubt he'd be poking everybody and saying, "Told you so."

So when the coach blows the conch shell for half time, parents and players alike collect themselves for a few minutes of civilized interaction. It's not unusual to hear a conversation between moms take a distinct tonal turn when play resumes for the second half:

"... so I was explaining to Tiffany that if she is more patient with her little brother ... KICK THE BALL—SLAM INTO 'EM—MAKE 'EM SORRY THEY CAME—SEND 'EM HOME TO THEIR BARBIES ... that he'd be more likely to comply with her wishes."

And the cheering has a sort of pattern. Much of it is chanted in series of three; i.e., "GET IT GET IT GET IT," "GO GO GO," and "SHOOT SHOOT SHOOT." And it goes in a sort of wave, like a crescendo and decrescendo. As the team passes along the sidelines, the swell of verbalization follows it down the field. So once again, we see a kind of rhythmic similarity to the fire-ring rituals of our predecessors.

There's further evidence in the face-painting phenomenon we often observe in crowds of fans at professional football games. And aren't pompoms just modern man's synthetic answer to shaking dried gourds and shrunken heads?

But I'm getting a bit off track here. As a very direct, socially-efficient, and somewhat retentive fellow at a party—where-he was-apparently-the-self-appointed-conversation-police-and evidently-felt-I-was-guilty-of-rambling-on-and-on-endlessly-without-purpose—I-wonder-where-he-got-that-silly idea—once asked me—"Is there a point to this?"

Yes sir, now as always, I do indeed have a point. But at present I forget what it is.

So anyway, just remember when you're sitting on the sidelines and you catch yourself yelling something you would normally be embarrassed to say even in one of those dreams you know is only a dream, fret not. It is normal and healthy behavior and quite acceptable as long as you don't go over the top and use words like "kill," "maim," or "dismember," or any type of profanity. Because if you do, you have violated the kids' sports fan's code of ethics, and you will be glared at by your fellow yellers like your hair's on fire or like they'd like to set it on fire, and you'll never feel the impulse to do it again—unless you're one of those boneheads whose mouth malfunctions as soon as your hiney makes contact with a bleacher seat. My advice to you is to get treatment.

The rest of us are perfectly normal.

## *Tough Love Wimps Out*

Disclaimer: The following column is the result of a teeth-gnashing, knee-jerking, steam-blowing frenzy that doesn't necessarily reflect the views of any particular parent or even the columnist, herself, in her post-implosion state.

Caution: Don protective gear and stand at a safe distance.

TEENAGERS ARE RATS. Beady-eyed, yellowed-toothed, sneaky little rodents. They bite the hands that feed them, and then ask for more. And though it's completely illogical, we love them more than life itself. Go figure.

At the time my kids were born, I thought labor and delivery were simply a physiological necessity, the act of a desperate baby struggling against resistance forces to get out of a tight spot. Now I realize they were foreshadowing, part of a master plan to hint at the agony of the teen years, when kids are struggling toward the independence of adulthood against the resistance of their parents. Only this is no twelve hour stint. This is seven years worth of dilating and contracting. One tends to get a bit prickly.

In a nutshell (that I could easily crack between my teeth at the moment), what all this means is that what a teenager finds to be the most fun thing to do is precisely the thing he's not supposed to do. This could range from speaking to you, the parent, as if you were the most primitive form of pond algae, to knocking over a Seven-Eleven. Most of our little lambkins fall somewhere in the mid-range.

Then comes the hard part, the responsibility we bear as disciplinarians. Though our first impulse may be a firing squad or maybe drawing and quartering, we must face the supreme challenge of meting out the most appropriate punishment for the particular infraction.

Personally, I've never encountered a more difficult task than this. Granted, I'm not an astrophysicist, but I'd wager what's left of my sanity that even a lion tamer would name disciplining his teenager his biggest source of stress. And it's not something that gets easier with experience. I feel more qualified to conduct a performance of the Boston Pops.

There are several reasons for this. One of them is the way kids respond to punishment. Generally, they don't like it. A favorite at my house is the righteous indignation response. How dare we infringe upon their basic freedom as teenagers to defy our authority! They act as if we should be brought before an international court for human rights violations.

Another problem is the inconsistency in disciplinary measures among parents. What if you've grounded your kid for a month, and his partner in crime gets a one week ban on Fruit Loops? Your darling just loves to hear about how he'll thank you for it someday.

Also, remember we're dealing with probably the most indulged generation in history. They can do things we find unforgivable in a friend or associate and then look at us with those puppy dog eyes and we're back to pinching their cheeks and putting extra fruit roll-ups in their lunches. We think they're so darn cute, and they know it.

The other thing they know is what gives them their real power. We want them to be *happy*. If they drag around like hopelessly dispirited shadows of their former selves, we feel like we've ruined their lives—the ultimate crime against humanity.

Well, guess what? Not me, not this time, not no how. I'm

mad as heck and I'm not going to take it anymore. The responsibility for setting my kid straight sits squarely on my husband's and my shoulders, and we're not going to back down from it.

So here it is: No extra fruit roll-ups for a month and a week of kitty litter duty. It has to hurt or it won't work.

Now excuse me while I go pinch some cheeks.

*All Critters Dear and Despicable*

## *Shedding Some Misconceptions About Man's Best Friend*

DON'T GET ME WRONG. I love my dog. He's the most unfailing giver of unconditional love I've ever known. But spring shedding season gives new meaning to the term "warm fuzzies."

My home this time of year is so effected by the dog's shedding that everything in it has a sort of airbrushed quality. It's not unlike a painting from the Renaissance period. I, myself, appear almost Raphael-esque when I look in the mirror. Who needs Retin-A? There's nothing like a fog of airborne dog hair to minimize those tiny lines and wrinkles.

We've got balls of what we affectionately call "tumbleweed" rolling across our floors and accumulating in the corners. If we diligently harvested them we'd have enough to stuff a mattress in no time.

Raleigh's tail contributes more than its share to the fallout. We try to avoid triggering his manic mood swings inside the house because when his tail wags, anyone in close proximity is transformed into a fur-bearing animal. If you happen to be standing on his tail when he gets up to walk away, you're left with a protein pompom under your shoe. And there's no end to it. He has an infinite supply. Maybe the Rogaine people should study the mysteries of canine hair replenishment. There could be hope for millions in dog tail transplants.

A pair of black wool pants is a pet hair magnet. I've been tempted to throw modesty to the wind and dress for work in the driveway, but once I climb into the minivan, it's all over. It's as bad as the house. I still arrive looking like I'm wearing a pelt.

For some reason, a doggie outing in the van sets off the shedding mechanism bigtime. Hairs seem to shoot out from his hide like quills from a porcupine. When I look in the rearview mirror, I see an excited, bewhiskered face framed in a billow of flying fur. We can travel hundreds of miles from home without Raleigh, but we always take a part of him with us.

So what's the solution? Don't tell me to get rid of the dog. I'd sooner have the hubby and kids draw straws for who goes, but the dog stays.

I suppose I could brush him more. But to be truthful, that would fall on my list of priorities somewhere between alphabetizing my seed catalogs and arranging plastic container lids in order of graduated size. Actually, it would probably vie for importance with melting down soap remnants and molding them into one big bar. I don't trust anyone that Martha Stewart-ish. So, in turn, I suppose I consider my matted dog a reflection of my relaxed, trustworthy nature.

Besides, I'd have to brush him outside and I couldn't do that without first alerting the National Weather Service to broadcast an air quality advisory.

"Due to dog brushing in the northwest sector, the air quality index is expected to be in the danger zone for persons with respiratory difficulties. You are cautioned to remain indoors or wear surgical masks if you must venture out between the hours of ______ and ______. We will keep you updated as the situation progresses."

A friend of mine just got a new puppy and he's suspiciously fluffy. She's always commenting on how pretty his coat is. I'm glad she likes it because before long, it's going to make up the bulk of her interior decor. She'll be hard pressed to recall her original color scheme. When someone asks the name of her decorator, the answer will be easy: Butch.

But she doesn't care, and neither do I. We're just a couple of suckers for a cold nose and a sloppy lick. That unconditional love thing'll get you every time.

I guess I'll just have to do some good old-fashioned, spring housecleaning. Maybe what I'll do is put on my black wool pants and do a few laps around the house. No self-respecting dog hair could resist them.

# *Of Pigs and Prophets*

IT'S THE SAME EVERY YEAR. I call it the Prince-and-the-Pauper Syndrome. I saw it coming ten years ago. My son pulled a few matchbox cars out of the toe of his Christmas stocking while, not far away, his best friend awoke to the sound of engines roaring in his bedroom. His parents had constructed a fully mechanized scale model of the Indianapolis 500 with his bed as the infield.

Woe is me. So it falls to those of us with more conservative spending styles to explain to our kids why their friend got a home theater installed in her bathroom so she could take in the latest video whilst percolating in the jacuzzi tub, while our darlings got rubber duckies, crazy foam, and loofahs.

How does one create an appreciation for a deluxe windshield scraper with padded grip and nylon brush when the neighbor kid gets a midnight blue Viper equipped with a centuple CD player with programming capability for trips to and from school for the next five months?

Here's what we do. We invite our children to sit cross-legged on the floor with us as we explain to them just how a Spartan existence such as ours builds character. We tell them that we intentionally don't spend megadollars on them at Christmas because we believe it will promote spiritual growth and development of inner strength, thus creating a sense of personal fulfillment. And we're cheap.

But we're quick to remind them that just because we don't sink big bucks into their Christmas presents doesn't mean we love them any less than those other parents who lavish their kids. Then we call them weedhoppers because we don't remember their names, pat them on their enlightened little heads, and send them off to play with rocks and sticks and other things of nature.

Oh yeah. And this year our little talk concluded with the presentation of the most meaningful Christmas gift ever. "Do not fret, fruits of our respective loin and womb," my husband and I told them, "for we have lovingly and intuitively selected for you something that will bring you countless hours of pleasure. Something that will heighten your awareness of the joy and inner peace to be found in simplicity."

And we unveiled the guinea pig.

They were stunned. Speechless. Overcome with emotion.

But once the element of surprise wore off, they began to bond with Wesley (that's the guinea pig's name) and, I believe, to learn some valuable life lessons from him. Imagine, a humble creature like a guinea pig bestowing the wisdom of the ages on one preteen and two teenagers who are treading dangerously close to the junk-culture chasm of the 1990's. Fur ball philosophy is a wondrous thing.

For example:

- You don't need a jacuzzi to keep yourself clean.
- If you eat plenty of veggies, you'll have bright eyes, shiny hair, and energy to burn into the wee hours.
- Sometimes an entertainment center can consist of no more than an empty toilet paper roll.

But most importantly:

- Even with the most modest of material possessions, you can be healthy, happy, command an enthusiastic approach to life, and be darn cute all at the same time.

In fact, the kids love that little guy so much they've made all kinds of plans for upgrading his accommodations. They want to make it into a sort of bi-level guinea pig condo with mirrors, exercise wheels, a padded bed and lots of colorful, fancy toys. He's one lucky pig. I'm telling you, he's going to be spoiled rotten.

Hey, wait a minute ...

## *Household Under Siege—De-tails Fuzzy*

A FEW DAYS AGO I gave in to the kids' demands for a kitten. After all, we were down to a dangerously low pet count of three, the lowest it's been in years. It was entirely too much to ask the kids to function in such a weakened state. An infusion of new blood was critical to their emotional health. Besides, we needed more animal hair on the carpet. You could almost tell what color it was.

Okay, let's get it over with. All together on the count of three. 1–2–3: "SUCKER!"

I don't know what came over me. Maybe I cracked under the constant wheedling. Maybe it's because the kids play me like a fine-tuned fiddle. Or maybe it's because they "borrowed" the little guy from the neighbors, plunked him into my lap, and he stared up at me with those huge, aren't-I-just-so-cute-you'd-let-me-scratch-the-heck-out-of-your-couch eyes. Whatever the cause, I obviously have no immunity. Someone should invent a vaccine.

So he's here to stay—all six inches of him (not including the tail). And a dynamic six inches it is. He has single-pawedly turned the balance of power in the household upside down. Just a tip to revolutionaries—if you're planning to stage a coup, I strongly suggest introducing a kitten into the current regime. It'll blow things wide open.

Lizzie, our senior resident cat and veteran of a guinea pig invasion and multiple incursions from visiting critters, has been reduced to a mere shadow of her former self. She, though usually in hiding, can occasionally be spotted lurking in a dark corner casting furtive glances around the room before making a mad dash for her food bowl or the litter box. Clearly, she feels her life is in peril. I keep telling myself her former, arrogant posture will return once she adjusts to the new order.

Raleigh, senior resident dog and commander-in-chief of all pets on the premises by virtue of his courage and outstanding leadership qualities, has been adopted by the new arrival as his surrogate mother. Having among his other admirable traits the patience of Job, the poor dog has managed thus far to keep a stiff upper lip in the face of this embarrassing turn of events. The kitten climbs him like a mountain, curls into the crook of his leg to sleep, and bats at his whiskers and chews on the pads of his feet to play. So far, the only time Raleigh has drawn the line was when the kitten fished around his soft underside to nurse. Bear in mind Raleigh is a male, and as such, vehemently defends his right of dominion over his privates.

The up side is that our new addition is very affectionate. And that's usually a very sweet and engaging characteristic in a pet. It does, however, become a bit tiresome at times—for example when I'm in a hurry to get ready to go somewhere and he keeps shinnying up my leg like it's a tree trunk. I've learned to overcome this inconvenience by doing sort of an Elvis-legs maneuver that keeps him floor-bound. Sometimes it's a little difficult to apply mascara, but I have to remind myself that from adversity, we grow.

So I guess we're all undergoing a lot of personal growth around our house these days. And we have our darling new kitten to thank for it.

There now. Don't you wish you had a character-building new pet in your home? I guess we can't all be so lucky. And who knows? Maybe I'll end up getting a new couch out of it.

## *The Buzzwords: Make My Day*

I HEREBY DECLARE WAR on those low-life, perverted, scum-sucking, excrement-brained wasps that stalk me and mine around every turn, at all hours of the day and night, in every imaginable location short of Saddam Hussein's secret underground bunker (which is not a place I frequent anyway), through summer and fall, every blessed year of my tortured existence, and probably will until my dying day.

But I'm cool. I'm not losing it. I'm just knee-jerking a little.

Admittedly, this last attack nearly pushed me over the edge. There I was, doing my momly duty with the noblest of intentions. I was at my daughter's soccer game, showing my support and exchanging astute tidbits of coaching strategy with the other moms, when one of the buzzing brutes flew up my shorts and stung me *very* high on the inner thigh. Now, NO ONE goes there without my permission. In fact, admission is a very selective process, and only those with high-level security clearance, medical or marital, need even make an attempt.

I felt so … violated. And now I'm obsessed with revenge. I've got a swatter in every room and one in my van, straight pins for impaling, and tweezers for de-winging and dismembering. I'm the Marquis de Sade of the bug world. I'm their worst nightmare. I plan to launch an assault the likes of which will send the ugly little striped buggers screaming in terror back to South America or whatever third world hive they came from. Maybe they'll even seek shelter in Hussein's bunker. Now, there's a marriage of like souls.

And I know I'm not alone. The atrocities are occurring at a staggering rate. I've heard tales of terror from soccer fields, county fairs, ball parks, and other bastions of wholesome Americana from sea to shining sea.

One of the most hair-raising stories just happened to involve my ... uh, a friend of mine whose name I will not use here because of the traumatic and somewhat embarrassing nature of the incident.

Picture this: An exceptionally adorable two-year-old boy (or it could be a girl, too, I suppose) sat dutifully on his miniature potty, proud of his new skill. He finished, pulled up his pants, and ran to tell Mommy what a marvelous thing he had done. Then, without warning, he was cruelly struck down in mid run by a horrific sting to his tender posterior.

Talk about negative reinforcement. The potty process was set back light years, and the child in question was forced to spend the afternoon lying on his stomach, derriere exposed, with a big glob of baking soda paste perched thereon. At least that's what I'm told.

Now, I ask you, can we continue to allow our children to be victimized by those who prey upon innocent flesh? No, I say! I, for one, am fighting back. In fact, I've become quite proficient at swatting these aces of agony in mid air with such force that they become embedded in the wall on the opposite side of the room. They could pass for bullet holes. Eliot Ness, eat your heart out. My swatter smokes.

And I encourage you, too, to arm yourselves. Take those swatters and cans of bug spray onto the fields of battle. Wear netting if you have to. Who cares if you look like a mutant Rambo—you'll be fighting the good fight for the welfare of all our loved ones. Together we can rid our community, state, and country of this insidious threat to the American way of life.

This is my quest.

See you at the soccer field. You can't miss me. I'll be in paramilitary garb, a gleam tinged with madness in my eye. The Exterminator.

## *New Tricks? Who's Doing the Teaching?*

My dog is losing the hair on one side of his head. He looks a little lopsided. I've been tempted to comb a flap over from the other side to cover the bald spot but decided if it doesn't bother him, it shouldn't bother me. Besides, he never hangs out in singles bars or wears gold chains, so why encourage that kind of vanity? The hairy chest is enough.

Anyway, the uneven hair loss has me puzzled. The only experience I've had with this sort of thing was when Ferdinand (ficticious name for my eldest child and heir to my vast fortune) was a baby. He, too, lost all the hair on one side of his head, but I think this was because he always lay on the same side in his crib, and it all just rubbed off. It didn't matter. I still thought he was the most beautiful thing I'd ever seen. Symmetry wasn't a critical factor to my devotion, and my friends kept tactfully mum about it.

But I would have to say my dog looks ridiculous. I still love him, of course, but there's no doubt that any hope of his modeling for a Precious Pooch calendar is out the window.

The problem is that he's getting old, and some very wacky things are beginning to happen to his body. (I can relate.) For example he's vocalizing a lot more than he used to. Anytime he moves or adjusts his position, he groans like a cold engine. He yips in his sleep. He communicates excitement, alarm and frustration with a highly developed dog vocabulary necessitated by his diminishing physical capabilities.

And speaking of physical capabilities, we're not seeing a lot of frenzied tail wagging these days. It too often throws him off balance. His front and back halves frequently appear to function independently of each other. Hence, he's understandably reluctant to walk across the tile floor to his food bowl because of the unpredictability of his body parts. Even though the front half is fairly goal-directed, the back half often ends up in a kind of homebase slide into a pile of laundry. This obviously embarrasses him. Here's a guy who has endured everything from party hats to bubble baths without complaint but considers an uncontrollable skid into a dirty sock drift a profound loss of dignity. Can you blame him?

Then there are the cataracts, the fatty tumors, and the broken-off teeth. It doesn't take a trained eye to see this is one patchy-coated, wizened old woofer. But to me, he's a blue ribbon grand champion.

I used to wonder why people kept decrepit old dogs around. After all, they couldn't play much, didn't offer any protection to speak of, and certainly weren't very decorative. They just lay around like lumps and occasionally bestowed upon their devoted owners a tired flop of the tail. What good was that?

I'm a little wiser now. Let me share with you some of what I've learned from my dog:

- A sloppy lick on the face of a child can banish a whole day's worth of boo-boos, internal and external.
- A warm, furry body makes a great pillow when you're stretched out on the floor reading or watching TV.
- A bright-eyed, tail-wagging greeting at the door eases the stress of a rough day and the burden of a heavy heart.
- The look of absolute trust and unconditional affection in those soft brown eyes boosts confidence and restores self esteem.
- A fuzzy, nonjudgemental ear encourages purging of the soul and healing of the spirit.

• A cold nose pressed into the palm of the hand is a promise of lifelong loyalty and enduring friendship.

These are gifts one doesn't soon forget.

So my dog may not look like much to the casual observer, but to honor a well-used maxim, beauty is in the eye of the beholder. And this particular beholder has never seen a more magnificent mutt.

## *Making a Mountain out of a Mouse Tale*

THIS WEEK'S COLUMN HAS ALL BUT WRITTEN ITSELF. It's a case in which truth is funnier than fiction, which is not to say I usually fictionalize things that I write about, but sometimes I might kind of jazz 'em up a little. Maybe just a smidge.

Anyway, this thing that happened—which I'll get to in just a minute, so don't get your knickers in a twist—is so utterly ridiculous I have no choice but to write about it. It's a no-brainer, which is great because my brain's in Florida for spring break. And the beauty of it is I don't have to embellish or exaggerate the slightest bit to jazz it up. Here's what happened:

I was nearly killed by a mouse last week.

I *mean* it. My daughter, whom I'll call Minnie in keeping with the rodent theme of this piece, was in the process of putting on a pair of soccer shoes that had been stored in the garage over the winter. I was tooling along behind the wheel of Floyd, my partially pink minivan, when suddenly Minnie let out an estrogen-curdling scream and launched into hysterics of the fire-ants-in-the-underwear variety. It startled me so much I nearly lost control and killed us both in a blazing crash. Thankfully, I was able to regain control of the vehicle due to the superior training I received in panic management as a passenger when Minnie's older brother and sister were learning to drive.

Once we'd pulled over and stopped, Minnie calmed down just enough to tell me there was a mouse in her shoe.

Apparently she'd tried to put it on and felt something in it, so she'd reached in and pulled out a live mouse. This bothered her. A lot. Hence, the screaming. Hence, too, the attempt on our lives.

When I asked her where the mouse went when she dropped it, she answered shakily from between her knees which were drawn up into the fetal position on the seat. The mouse had run up under the dash board.

Well, isn't *that* special, I thought. Now we could expect one of two things: either it would stay up there and get fricasseed in the engine or dart out and dance with wild abandon across our feet when I started driving and we'd have to take our chances with the fiery crash scenario again. Wonderful.

But if there's one thing I've learned, it's that a mom's gotta do what a mom's gotta do. And the other thing I've learned is that through rain, sleet, snow, or mouse attack, you can't miss soccer practice. So we bravely continued our journey to the field; Minnie, twitching and whimpering, and I, driving with my tippy-toes.

On the way, I remembered a friend telling us about how a mouse ran up under the dash of his daughter's car, died, and began to smell like something would that had crawled into a hot, confined space and died.

"Like athletic shoes?" I asked.

"Worse," he said.

Consequently, he'd taken the car apart, been unable to find the mouse, put the car back together, gotten a geo-thermo-nuclear-powered, long-range, target-sighting vacuum apparatus, and ultimately sucked the corpse out of the system via the tailpipe. Sort of a mousectomy. He said the mouse hit the holding tank of the vacuum weapon with an immensely satisfying "Thunk," and the family celebrated their independence with feasting, dancing, and mock mouse battles for a week.

Again, I remind you I'm not exaggerating.

In light of this, I knew something had to be done soon, before old Mickey migrated into the bowels of the van.

When we got to the field, I barely had time to put it in park before we both dove out the doors and rolled to our feet, commando style. That's when another soccer mom, whose initials are M.M. so I'll call her Mighty Mouse, entered the scene. Once Mighty Mouse ascertained the difficulty, she started poking around under the dashboard, her face not two feet from the murderous beast. I'm telling you, the woman has nerves of steel. She fearlessly prodded with a rake handle, a lacrosse stick, and her own hand wrapped in nothing but a 100% cotton, non-shrink T-shirt. Eventually, her hand thus wrapped, she was able to grab the mouse and fling him through the air onto the grass beside the parking lot.

Observing from about thirty feet away, sitting in her car with her seat belt on, another soccer mom screamed. Mighty Mouse tossed me the T-shirt, gave a devil-may-care chuckle, and said, "Good thing she had her seat belt on." Then she swaggered to her car and drove off into the sunset. What a woman. No exaggeration.

In conclusion, I'd like to point out that there's an important lesson to be learned from all this. In matters of mice and men, some of us must face the fact that we're just plain spineless. So if the shoe fits, wear it.

But shake it out first.

*Annoyances —Fingernails*
*On the Chalkboard of Life*

## A Common Cooking Whine

TWO HOURS OF A TYPICAL WEEK NIGHT at my house:

5:45 Drop off child #2 at cheerleading practice.

6:00 Drop off child #3 at soccer.

6:15 Rush home to whip up a nutritious home-cooked meal à la Martha Stewart. Start chopping veggies for well-intentioned stir fry.

6:20 Phone rings. "Is (child #2) there?"
"No, sorry. She's at cheerleading."
"Okay, thanks." Hang up. Resume chopping.

6:25 Phone rings again. Chop a little fingertip into mix. Oh well, protein. Answer phone, sucking finger.
"Hello, Mrs. Dittoe?"
"Yes?"

"This is Sally with Mothers for Cleaner Public Restrooms, and —"

I tell her I'm a little busy, but I'd be delighted to call her back at home during *her* dinner hour, and we can chat then.

6:30 Let the dog out and the cat in.

6:31 Dump veggies in wok, still hopeful I can pull this family meal thing off. Put on water for rice. Get out stuff for salad.

6:40 *Brrrng!* Cheerily the phone beckons me.
"Good evening. Mrs. Dittoe?"
"Yeah?" warily.

"This is Jesse with Mohave Basement Waterproofing (no pause) do you have a minute (no pause) good (no pause) let me tell you about —"

"Excuse me," I cut in, "I happen to be the national president of the Save the Spore Foundation, a non-profit group of concerned citizens dedicated to the protection of endangered mildews and fungi, primarily those found in the lower levels of private residences. May I have your full name and that of your immediate supervisor?"

Click. Works every time.

6:50 Child #1 dashes in, grabs a banana and a bag of chips, and runs out saying he's going to the soccer game at the high school. I say "Hi" about the same time the door slams shut.

6:55 *Brrrng!* "Hello, this is Raphael with Wutta Pane Replacement Windows. May I ask how old your home is?

"Sure, but I won't tell you. We don't need your windows, and you might be an enemy agent. We live in a subterranean bomb shelter to protect us from imminent nuclear devastation, invasion by extraterrestrials, and the infiltration of robo-people sent by third world powers to move incognito among those who walk naively above ground."

Click. I love that one.

7:00 Let the dog in.

7:02 *Brrrng!* "Is (child #1) there?"

"No, he's at the soccer game."

"Thanks." Click.

7:05 The rice boils over, leaving a brown, crusty ring on the burner.

7:08 *Brrrng!* "Is this the lady of the house?"

"No, this is the raving lunatic of the house, poised to go off on the next person who asks me for money on the phone."

Click.

7:15 Give up on salad. Open a jar of apple sauce and plunk a spoon in it.

7:17 *Brrrng!* More pleas from telemarketing purgatory.

"Hi, this is Jerry with [insert name of major credit card here]. I'm calling to tell you about our exciting new insurance coverage for family pets. Do you have any of those beloved, furry family members dwelling with you? And if so, wouldn't you be interested in hearing how they can be insured in much the same way as their human counterparts?"

"Let me tell you something, Mr. Cute and Cuddly. Not only am I not interested, but if I had a gun in my hand right now, I'd pump six rounds into the phone."

Click. No more Mrs. Nice Guy.

7:20 Remove the wok full of crispy critters from the stove.

7:30 Pick up children #2 and #3 at respective practices.

7:40 Child #1 comes breezing in.

7:42 Everyone sits at the table staring at a platter of cinders, a bowl with a globular clump of rice in it, and a jar of apple sauce. They turn basset-hound faces toward me.

7:43 I vent. "What do you expect? Duck à l'Orange? Bouillabaisse? I've been defending the fortress from aliens attacking via phone for the last two hours. Give me a break!" I jerk my thumb over my shoulder. "There's bologna in the fridge. If you want me I'll be in my bomb shelter."

7:44 I limp off to the bedroom to lick my wounds.

7:45 *Brrrng!* I overhear my husband say, "Sorry, not interested."

You'd think he could be a little more creative.

## *Technical Support Services: Direct Line to the Divine*

LATELY, WHEN I'VE SAID MY BEDTIME PRAYERS, right up there with the first-string players like world peace and an end to hunger is "please don't let my computer go down."

I admit it, it's a little selfish in the scheme of things, but at least I've moved beyond my more youthful requests for enhanced personal development ... of the physiological sort. That was back in the Barbie years. What I was granted was the awareness that the value of a person is more than the sum of her physical attributes, and I'm thankful for that lesson. It frees me to concern myself with life's greater issues.

Like my stupid computer. How humbling it is to be diminished to complete helplessness by an arrogant little piece of hardware. Again, a lesson: Woman, or man for that matter, is not invincible, despite Helen Reddy's claims to the contrary.

So there I sat, staring at a dialogue box on my computer screen that said something like, "Cannot run program. Run from original application, you fool." And nowhere in my computer books, which are written in some dead Byzantine language, could I find a similar message or how to respond.

My natural conclusion was that one of the computer cretins I live with had been monkeying around with my delicate machine. Upon investigating, I found that no one else had used the computer for a couple of days. I was the computer cretin. My humility index rose further.

Okie-dokey, thought I. I'll call the technical support number at *Computers-(backwards R)-Sadistic* listed in my otherwise useless computer books.

Ha! First I was instructed to push one of half a dozen buttons on my touch-tone phone for the appropriate extension. Then I was told to do it again. And again. Now, I don't remember much from my math classes about exponential multiplication, but my guess is that this vast network of extensions branching off *Computers-(backwards R)-Sadistic's* main number could accommodate half the population of Cleveland at any given time. And I was just one more gnat flapping futilely in the web.

For the apparent purpose of keeping me mollified, a recorded message ran every fifteen seconds telling me that I, along with half of Cleveland, was a "valued customer" and my call was "important" to them, so to please "remain on the line for the next available representative." To rub salt in the wound, the message was grammatically incorrect. My fillings were beginning to feel as if I were chewing aluminum foil.

After twenty minutes of this torture (what do they do to the customers they *don't* value—make them listen to a medley of Ross Perot's greatest campaign spots?), I had doodled through my tablet of paper and was carving the counter top.

The electronic imbecile thanked me for my patience for the eightieth time, and then it hit me: What was I doing to myself? There it was nearly noon and I was sitting at the kitchen counter still in my robe, with the phone stuck to my ear, hair cowlicked in every direction, chewing my cuticles, and defacing the formica. How could I have let a lousy piece of machinery reduce me to this?

And suddenly I realized ... It was up to *me* to overcome this problem—up to *me* to find a solution. And I knew that the response to my nightly prayer was to throw me a road block which, in circumventing, would make me a stronger, more confident person.

Empowered, I took the bull by the horns and called my former computer class instructor to come bail me out. In no time at all, he rode in on his white steed and slew the computer dragon. At this point, I would've been willing to give him my firstborn in payment, but he asked only a nominal fee for his services. Though I really pressed the firstborn thing (a seventeen year old boy), he graciously, but firmly, assured me that money would suffice and rode off into the sunset to save another poor soul from a user-friendly wolf in sheep's clothing.

I had done it. I had looked the computer demon in the eye and had the courage to hire someone to vanquish it.

That night in my prayers, I gave thanks for another lesson learned and a fear conquered. Now I can move to more important issues.

Cellulite's a fairly universal problem, don't you think?

## *It's Over When the Out-of-Tone Lady Sings*

WHERE ARE YOU STATIONED for the Great Radio War? Is your family fighting with frequency or just giving you a little static?

Forgive the puns, but my family's bickering over the car radio has me tuned to FM—feeble-minded.

It starts as soon as we head out the door to go somewhere.

"Shotgun!" somebody yells. Translated, that means "I get to sit in the front seat and control the radio." They couldn't care less about the view from up there. Power's the thing. Shotgun is a misnomer. It should be something like AK-47, the way the person in control uses his position to assault the rest of us with his music preferences.

And what's worse is how frequently the radio-control person, or designated tuner if you will, feels compelled to change the station. My kids station surf. It's nerve-racking. As soon as a song's over, they're on the prowl for another one they like. What's wrong with kids today? Is it the instant gratification thing? When I was a kid, I had a favorite station I listened to. It was a loyalty issue. And putting up with the DJ's ramblings and the endless commercials just seemed like the polite thing to do. I think this hopping from station to station is symbolic of the general lack of discipline among the youth of today. Maybe military school's the answer.

Volume's another problem. Heaven knows we've got enough of it without the radio, but it's not as if everyone stops talking when the radio's on. They just talk over it. And the more kids we get in the van, the higher they crank it up. Then they yell over it. They seem to feel that bellowing over a good beat enhances the quality of their communication. What it enhances is the quality of my headache.

And do you think it's the owner and operator of the hard-working pink and burgundy minivan who gets to set the buttons on the radio for the stations she prefers? Wake up and smell the Clearasil, baby. I've put up with everything from the Citrusheads to the Gourd Smashers for the past several years, but do you think they can deal with a little shot of NPR once in a while? The way they squeal, you'd think it was auditory torture. It doesn't matter that I've endured, in total, thirty-plus hours of labor and delivery, changed approximately 16,425 diapers, wiped more goopy noses than I care to remember, and dealt with enough adolescent attitude to bring an American Gladiator to his knees, I apparently don't rate a measly radio station button in my own van. More symbolism of the times. Makes me wonder how much control I really have in this parenting process and how much is merely an illusion.

Whining aside for a moment, I'd like to share an informative little tidbit with you. Did you know that studies indicate listening to classical music makes people more intelligent? Supposedly it boosts your brain power. I toyed with the idea of keeping this little gem to myself so my kids would always score at the high end of the grading curve, but once again my journalistic integrity won out. I decided to enlighten my fellow parents for the greater good of today's youth, undisciplined little radio station-grubbing ingrates that they are. Besides, I figured you wouldn't have any better luck getting your kids to listen to it than I have.

This, in turn, suggests that perhaps other types of music can effect our mental processes and aptitudes. For example, maybe country music improves our ability to operate large machinery. Perhaps listening to Top '40s stimulates our interest in current events. And rap music, possibly, subconsciously motivates us to install home security systems.

But back to the issue at hand—winning the war of the radio. You've got a few options here; fight back, surrender, or engage in a little psychological warfare. I'm going to try the latter. My plan is to learn all the lyrics and drive the kids around town with the windows down, belting out their favorite songs with great gusto for all to hear. I predict immediate and unconditional capitulation.

Who says I have to fight fair? I'm the mom.

## *Designs for Splashing Get Tongue-Lashing*

'Tis the season to buy a swimsuit. But, as we all know, they don't make swimsuits for women between the ages of thirty and seventy. Nothing exists between string bikinis and the style one might liken to a panel truck. Likewise, nothing exists within that framework between no cup and an accordion-puckered double-D. As if our attitudes about body image aren't suffering enough, we have to choose between no coverage and enough in the bra to accommodate our sunscreen, towel and beach umbrella as well as the kids' water wings. Who needs a beach bag?

Then there's the bottom half of the suit. Our choice there is full moon or total eclipse.

Could this be a conspiracy to keep us off the beaches and out of the public eye? No one can convince me that in this age of sheep-cloning a swimsuit can't be designed that would flatter a forty-five year old body.

I, unlike Farrah Fawcett and Dyan Cannon, do not wish to recreate my eighteen year old body. The same number of pounds do not arrange themselves in the same configuration on my frame as they once did. I just want some fashion designer to give me a suit that looks reasonable enough to wear in public. A suit that looks like a little more than a postage stamp and a little less like a shower curtain. Maybe the manufacturers aren't aware of the sunken treasure there is in middle-aged swimwear. I may not be a Barbiebody, but I'd be willing to shell out some major clams to look decent on the sand, as I suspect would many others in my age group.

I'm not striving for perfection. I gave up on that in a previous life. I know some things can't be helped. Every time I take in the rear view in the three-way mirror of a swimwear dressing room, I'm reminded there's no turning back. With the overhead lights casting shadows over every ridge and ripple, I regret that no one has invented body spackle. It's a painful indication that I'm in the process of returning to the earth and its elements; ocean legs and amber waves of grainy flesh. Ashes to ashes, dust to dust.

Maybe what we middle-aged lovelies should do is launch an organized protest—march through swimsuit departments with signs that say, "We Demand Representation" or write in lipstick on the three-way mirrors, "No Money for Minis and No Sales on Sails" or "Give Us the Right Stuff or We'll Swim in the Buff" ... well, maybe that's a little overboard.

But we need to unite and make waves! Form an advocacy group! Rage against the machine! Maybe we could call ourselves Synchronized Swimwearers.

Okay ... that's enough righteous indignation for one week. Now I'll get back to issues I feel less passionate about—most of which I confront fully clothed.

## *Dryer Does Double Duty as Slot Machine*

NOTHING BRINGS A FAMILY TO ITS KNEES faster than a major appliance going on the fritz. In our case it was the clothes dryer.

If you want to completely immobilize an active clan, cut off it's supply of clean underwear, T-shirts, and sports uniforms. The kids panicked. We had stuff hanging from every ledge inside and outside the house, spread all over the trampoline, and draped over the deck railing. We thought of appealing to the governor to send over the 'copters and declare us a disaster area so we'd qualify for aid. Then we could console ourselves with a trip to the mall for emergency provisions. I'm telling you, it was a toga party at the Dittoes, only not quite so festive. These things are more fun when they're voluntary.

So I called in my favorite repair person. This is a guy who's been with us through thick and thin, pulled us through the most harrowing repair situations, has personality to burn, always saves the day, and somehow leaves us smiling even as we write the check. He should run for president. He certainly instills more confidence than the Three Musketeers of '96. And he didn't laugh when he pulled a wad of pet hair the size of Rhode Island out of our refrigerator coils. He's got my vote.

Anyway Randall, I'll call him, did a preliminary examination and gave me a range of possible explanations from "not so bad" to "you're gonna have to scratch this year's vacation and buy a new dryer." One of them I think involved a belt, and the other was something that sounded to my penny-pinching ears like transfixation of the metamorphosed eunuch gladiator. *That* had an ominous ring.

Then he took out his surgical instruments and popped off the front cover of the dryer. It sounded like somebody hit the weekly jackpot at the Desert Inn (minus Wayne Newton's crooning in the background). About twenty dollars fell out of the dryer, ten or so in coin and a ten dollar bill that's been missing since my daughter's birthday that we've all, in turn, been accused of "borrowing." Not to mention at least fifteen dollars worth of buttons. It appears we've been running the largest money-laundering operation in the Midwest.

"Or maybe that's the problem," said Randall in his ultra-patient, almost fatherly, these-Dittoes-are-wacks tone of voice.

As it turned out, that was indeed the problem. And as Randall graciously accepted my thanks and check, he once again assured me not to worry, he'd seen worse. He always says that with such sincerity, even though I know he exerts enough self control to herniate internal organs until he can get into his truck, slam the door, and laugh himself senseless. The man is a pro.

So in closing, I'd like to offer a few helpful hints based on my extensive experience as to the washability of certain items commonly found, or not found, in pockets:

- Chapstick does well if it doesn't make it into the dryer.
- Paper money is far more durable than checks and remains quite spendworthy even if tumbled dry.
- Coins shine up nice as new.
- Stickers are forever if put through both machines.
- O.S.U. vs. Michigan football tickets disintegrate completely even if run only through the delicate cycle and, in so doing, will threaten even the strongest marital relationship.
- Library cassette tapes unravel and wrap around every item in the load, requiring hours of detangling and cost a minimum of seven dollars to replace.

One last thing. If you develop a problem with one of your appliances, I highly recommend Randall. If you have trouble reaching him, be patient. He'll probably be at my house. The refrigerator's on the blink again, and the cat's missing.

## *Ching-Ching, It's Spring!*

I'VE BEEN THINKING ABOUT HIRING a motivational speaker for my kids. Someone who'll roll up his shirt sleeves and work up a sweat convincing them that they're made of the right stuff to reach for the stars and master the universe and all that other inspiring stuff.

What am I yammering on about *now*? Am I referring to academic success, strength of character, achievement of goals, or spiritual commitment?

Don't be absurd. Anyone who's ever had a kid knows I'm talking about selling wrapping paper.

Spring and fall are the fund-raising seasons, and as surely as the earth will turn on its imaginary axis, kids' clubs and teams will declare these two seasons their times to raise the almighty moolah they need for their continued existence. It's an immutable law of nature. And I wholeheartedly support the effort—especially when the alternative is for the parents to make a sizable donation to the club's treasury.

But it's not getting any easier. When each of my kids was exposed to that first fund-raising opportunity (another entry for the baby book) at about kindergarten age, she attacked it with the fervor of a kid whose life wouldn't be complete without the highest-seller's incentive prize of a deluxe 3' by 3' dream playhouse made of genuine recycled cardboard. Her enthusiasm was boundless. Maybe kindergartners should hire out as motivational speakers.

But as the years went by, her energetic attitude toward selling high quality chocolates, four to a box, diminished. She became more listless and uninspired as her heap of colorful cardboard rewards grew ever higher.

And then her siblings got involved. The same neighbor could conceivably get three calls in one night from different Dittoes peddling everything from handy ribbon shredders to spicy salsa seasoning. People turned on their answering machines, hung blackout curtains, and hid under their beds.

One October—and this is as true or even truer than 50% of what I say in this column—we were operating *seven different* fund-raising campaigns out of our house. All legitimate. All for good causes. And none of which did anything to improve relations with friends and neighbors. Our relatives, of course, have no choice. They have to love us no matter what. They have to buy the stuff, too. It's written in blood.

Then there's the tit-for-tat thing. If I buy oranges from your kid, you have to buy cookies from mine. If you don't, you will violate the unwritten fund-raiser parents' code of ethics and your name will become non-decomposing landfill in supportive-parent circles. Hence, much of our kids' client lists are comprised of a high percentage of tit-for-tatters, those who live in fear of social persecution.

So as spring springs eternal and green sprouts signal the promise of life anew, get out your checkbook and prepare to open your door to a range of fresh young faces to older fund-raising zombies. It's all for deserving organizations. Be merciful and generous, as I shall to your little peddlers, being ever cognizant of social faux pas.

And if you have a kindergartner to recommend, I'll pay him big bucks to come and speak to my flagging sales crew, inspiring them to greater fund-raising heights.

Or maybe it would just be easier to make a donation to the club treasury.

## *Talkin' Trash about College Cash*

I SAID TO MY HUSBAND, "Let's set aside a couple hours tonight and spend some time alone together."

As I predicted, the hint of a romantic interlude drew him in. I had to talk pretty fast when he realized my intention was for him to help me fill out our son's financial aid forms for college.

He accused me of the old bait-and-switch maneuver. My offer to light candles and wear a teddy did little to assuage his irritation. He always gets a little peevish when he's forced to think about spending his life's savings on the first quarter of college for his eldest of three children. He's got this silly notion that college is unreasonably expensive. Men.

The couple of hours turned into four days. He looked like Rip Van Winkle when we were finished. The blush of my youthfulness had even paled slightly. (Picture Granny Clampett in a teddy.) It definitely put us a few steps closer to the grave.

What a monstrous experience—entirely appropriate for Halloween week. The little goblins who made out these financial forms came, figuratively tapping at the door of our financial well being, and said, "*Trick or Treat!*" Sure, they appeared cute and harmless, but from what our more experienced and destitute friends tell us, giving them a generous handful of our goodies is no guarantee they won't still soap the windows of our nest egg and stick-the-horn of our vacation fund. Then they'll toilet paper what remains of our savings and flush us down the drain of debt.

I'm not kidding about this. When we finally finished those forms, I felt like I'd undergone a four-day frisk. I felt violated. They probed all the nooks and crannies. They asked about our assets, our debts, our investments, the value of our home, the worth of our obnoxious little pink and burgundy minivan, the cost of counseling resulting from the trauma of driving it and how much was covered by insurance. They wanted to know about our kids' assets. I dumped out piggy banks and counted. I went to the genealogy department of the library and researched our ancestors' Civil War wages. I rented a U-Haul to transport tax returns dating back to the Mayflower to the financial aid detectives.

Then, I signed my name on the dotted line, swearing under potential penalty of caning or, in rare cases, beheading, that every answer I'd given was accurate to the nanopenny.

This is scary stuff. I haven't had a moment's peace since the whole business began. It's not only that I was tormented for days by the forms themselves, but living with ol' Rip hasn't exactly been a stroll through the edelweiss. He's still holding a grudge because what he thought was going to put a spring in his step ended up aging him twenty years. Telling him he looks distinguished only elicits a toothless sneer and a dagger-like glare from jaundiced eyes.

So, if you're about to undergo this vicious, life-sucking process, I have some advice for you: Hide all your money under your mattress first. I won't tell if you don't. And if my story, though it was painful to divulge, can save even one person from the nightmare I had to endure, my sacrifice will not have been in vain.

Good luck, my friend and comrade. If you need it, I have a teddy you can borrow.

## *I'm Dreaming of a Night Sniffless*

You know I don't like to whine, but ... well, at least I don't go on and on ... Okay, so I squeal like a *rusty hinge* when something's bothering me. Will you *please* let me make my point already?!

It's 3:00 in the morning, and here I sit writing this column instead of being nestled, all snug in my bed while visions of sugarplums dance through my head.

"And why is that?" you'd ask, if you had a compassionate bone in your body. I'll tell you why. Because Santa brought me a cold. I would have preferred a lump of coal, if the truth be known. But that jolly old elf slid down my chimney and dropped a little Christmas cootie on my defenseless, sleeping form.

I don't understand it—I've been good. Who can explain such a senseless act of virus?

Anyway, whenever I try to lie down, a little throat bugger wiggles a feather and makes me hack like I've got a hairball. He does this at very precise intervals because I've discovered I can fit exactly the chorus and one line of a verse of Linda Ronstadt's *Poor, Poor, Pitiful Me* between coughing fits.

The mind makes odd sport of sleeplessness.

And the cough syrup hasn't been invented that can help me. I hope daylight will bring a fresh perspective, because I'm almost desperate enough to consider battery acid or maybe even a neck tourniquet. But on second thought, daylight is about the time the throat bugger's shift is over, and I'll finally be able to get to sleep. That gives me about an hour before I awaken to the cheerful clatter of breakfast dishes piling up and the happy chatter of people with clear airways who got a solid eight hours who expect me to wash them … the dishes, that is.

That's the worst part of all. Nobody feels sorry for me. I'm not supposed to get sick. I'm the mom.

In a perfect world, I'd be lying on a silk fainting couch with a cool cloth on my head, while someone, preferably one of my concerned, doting offspring, spooned broth into my mouth as her siblings hovered about plumping my pillows and massaging the pressure points on my feet. (One can daydream. Heaven knows I'm not doing it in my sleep.)

I'm looking mighty fine, too. My nose is red and bulbous, my upper lip is swollen and chapped, and sleep deprivation has accessorized with puffy eye bags to complete the ensemble. A glance in the mirror yields the impression of W.C. Fields. My voice is reminiscent of Elmer Fudd, but I won't be chasing silly wabbits for a while because I'm moving like a slug in slo-mo.

Okay, so I'm indulging in industrial-strength whining. I suppose you'd be clicking away on your linoleum, doing Michael Flatley's Riverdance Workout. Nothing's more annoying at times like this than you type A's.

Since I've come this far, I might as well rant on and complete the cycle of complaint.

So I'll get up in the morning, drag around the house like a wet dish rag, and then just about the time, in early evening, when some oxygen has begun to seep into my brain, everything will shut down. My brow ridges, eye sockets, and cheekbones will start to feel like petrified sponge cake, and the whole process will begin again.

Don't be so smug. Those of us who have suffered at the hands of the holiday humbug (and I understand there are quite a few of us) may just be sleeping like babies next week when *you're* up counting flowers on the wallpaper and dripping like a faucet. The Christmas cootie may be coming your way even as you gloat, so how's about making with a little sympathy?

Some chicken soup would be nice. And my pillows sure could use a good plumping.

## *Summer Travelers Over a Barrel*

REMEMBER WHEN YOU WERE YOUNG and idealistic and when someone asked what you wanted to do with your life you gave answers that included such noble things as putting an end to hunger, curing disease, and working for world peace? Okay, now admit it. How many of you, if asked the same question today, would say you wish you would've invented the orange construction barrel? (What shameless capitalists you've become. Me, too.)

That guy has got to be in the chips big time. I really believe that if those things were placed side by side across the U.S., they would zig-zag through each of the 50 states (crossing the ocean floor where necessary) and encircle all major metropolitan areas with plenty left over for stacking in the median strip and overturning on the berm. In fact, I think someone is already conducting this study, perhaps the Institute for Interstate Idiocy, because I've done a lot of driving this summer and it looks like "Barrels Across America" out there. And there's very little evidence of actual construction taking place.

Maybe it's really a philanthropic effort of some sort—perhaps a campaign to heighten our awareness of some social ill like vehicular aggression, you know—people becoming angry about driving situations and reacting violently.

Well, guess what? IT'S NOT WORKING. Though I've never been one to carry a concealed firearm myself, I assure you I would giggle with glee if the guy in the car ahead of me took out a shotgun and blew away a few of the ugly things just for fun.

Maybe it's an advertising campaign perpetrated by the airlines to encourage people to travel by plane. I bet the endless string of orange barrels, viewed aerially, spell out messages like "Enjoy your flight" and "We look forward to serving you again."

And will someone please explain to me why it's always during the summer, when 99% of the population takes to the roads for family vacations, that these insidious cylinders squeeze traffic down to one creepy-crawly lane in each direction? It upsets the whole cycle of civilized society. It lengthens our travel time, reduces time spent at our destination, and thereby, cuts down on the time we have for relaxation and renewal. Then we travel back the same barrel-squeezed roadways cranky and resentful and return to our homes and jobs in the same unproductive, negative state of mind we left.

I don't want to overstate this, but these innocent (though obnoxious) looking neon obstacles could actually be *responsible* for many of society's ills. It's an angry world out there. I wonder how many psychotic criminals under psychoanalysis would look at Rorschach ink blots and see construction barrels cannibalizing unsuspecting minivans and campers.

Even if road construction is a necessary evil, there's got to be a better way of handling it. Something that would make travel delays more interesting and enjoyable. Like maybe stationing some of those nice ladies who do cooking demonstrations at every 10th barrel or so to hand out samples. Just imagine how cheering it would be, when you're stuck in traffic, if you rolled down your window and someone smiled and handed you a coupon and a cocktail weenie on a toothpick. Or there could be sno-cone vendors or puppet shows for the kids. Advertisers could even lease barrels the same way they do billboards—"Renaldo's Pasta Palace—Exit Right at 64th Barrel"—it could do wonders to reduce unemployment and boost free enterprise.

And if these things could actually improve the quality of your road travel time, you would be happier and more relaxed. You might even begin to think idealistic thoughts again. Like how ideal it would be to buy stock in orange barrel manufacturing.

## *Mayday! Mayday! Mom In Distress!*

OKAY. LET'S SEE A SHOW OF HANDS. How many of you have time to floss in May? I, for one, know I'm too darn busy when I don't observe a conscientiously applied program of oral hygiene.

I'm also not exercising or doing any leisure reading. The only sort of "fringe" activity I haven't given up because of my schedule is unwrapping the foil from the chocolate eggs I always sneak out of the kids' Easter baskets. It would take something really extreme to make me too busy to eat chocolate. Like maybe attempting to outrun an earthbound comet.

I've said it before and I'll say it again … if I can remember what it is. Oh yeah—May is the month from Hades. If this offends some of you, I'll apologize in June when I have more time. But right now, I'm not in my right mind. (*My right mind* being a concept that's hard to pin down in a normal calendar month, but elusive as a greased gecko in May.)

Due to the elevated sporting event and end-of-school-year activity count, I have no time to engage in some of the most menial tasks and bodily functions or, for that matter, even complete this senten …

May bonks me between the eyes every year like a champagne cork, taking me by surprise as if I'd never lived through it before. There is absolutely no way to prepare myself for it other than to remember the immortal words of the fictitious and unromantic late husband of Mrs. Doubtfire in the film by the same name, "Brace yourself, Effie!"

(And by the way, if you were able to read the previous sentence in one sitting, you have entirely too much time on your hands this month, and I hereby resent you. It took me three sittings to write it.)

There's no fighting it. May's a mess. Aside from the tulips and daffodils in my yard, which are a pleasant surprise because in my current mental state I don't remember planting them, there are a few tried and true ways I can tell it's May without looking at the calendar, which is a frivolous waste of time anyway.

Here are some of the undeniable signs of May at my house (and I suspect, at many of yours):

- We wear crinkled clothes because everything gets pulled out of the dryer, stuffed into a basket, and worn directly from there without benefit of folding or ironing.
- The carpet crunches because of a vacuuming deficiency.
- My flower gardens look like renaturalized prairies, as does my hair much of the time, both due to lack of grooming.
- To save time when I get dressed in the morning, I hold my underwear out in front of me and step into it as I'm walking. In May, not even underwear can be allowed to impede my forward progress, or it won't get worn.
- Dinners consist of casseroles left over from whatever spring banquet was held the previous night, which means we subsist on a diet of various types of noodles and brownies, my personal carry-in specialties. In other words, cuisine I can nail in 30 minutes or less.
- We lose contact with friends and loved ones. In June, we send word we've survived.
- A family dinner means on a TV tray with Tim "The Tool Man" Taylor's family.
- Floyd, my pink and burgundy minivan, smells like mildewed athletic equipment, and there's a jumble of damp, muddy rain gear behind the back seat.
- No one can find two shin guards, cleats, or soccer socks in the same place.

- There are muddy footprints—human, canine, and feline, but none mine—all over the floor.
- My windows don't sparkle.
- The van's always low on gas.
- I'm pooped.

Now if you'll excuse me I have to meet someone—myself, coming and going.

# *Theories and Epiphanies (And a Few Revelations From No-Woman's-Land)*

## *Just Say No*

LET'S SAY I'M IN A BEAUTY PAGEANT ... Okay, let's take it back a step further. Let's say we're on another planet where ridiculous things like that happen. For crying out loud, I'm just trying to set the stage for a hypothetical situation here. Gimme a break. If you prefer, we'll say I'm a game show contestant. Geez.

Anyway, Burt Parks or Bob Barker or somebody like that asks me what my hobbies are. Everyone else has said things like coin collecting or helping mankind, depending upon which scenario we're going with, and I'm desperately trying to come up with a hobby because I'm a middle-aged mother of three teenagers and I don't have a life.

"Arguing with my kids," I blurt out, realizing I've just flushed away any shot I had at the crown, and in the game show format there's an embarrassed hush while the host attempts to recover his dimples and move on.

It is such a confession of inadequacy to admit you argue with your kids. It's like going public with an admission that you buy generic. It's social suicide.

But no more dirty little secrets for me. I'm coming clean. I'm looking at it as the first step in my recovery.

When the kids were little, they were what we proudly called "very verbal." We actually encouraged it. Can you imagine? Someone once told me my kid would never have to use his fists because he could always talk his opponents into submission.

(I'm not telling you which kid because he'd be embarrassed. That's the way the first born is.)

But my arguing hobby stops now. I'm corking the bottle, pulling the plug, damming the river. No more of the old "very verbal" at the Dittoes. I'm taking up needlepoint.

Why? Because the experts now say—and I have the utmost respect for all experts because of their official title of *expert* which even in the absence of childrearing experience is an awe-inspiring thing—that, and hear this well, WE SHOULDN'T ARGUE WITH OUR KIDS.

Now, I have to tell you, ever since I heard this inspiring message I've been repeatedly striking my forehead with the palm of my hand and saying, "Gee, why didn't *I* think of that?"

*We shouldn't argue with our kids.*

So simple yet so profound. It all sparkles with crystal clarity now. I can't believe I wasted all those years on reasoning and explanations. I feel like such a ninny.

I can't begin to imagine how this new approach will simplify my life.

"Mom, may I go to the mall Saturday and hang out there until it closes?"

"No, you may not."

"But why not?"

"I'm sorry. This issue is not up for debate."

Then magically, the child will stop talking, shrug his shoulders, and walk away instilled with a new spirit of cooperation. And if you're especially skilled at your refusal technique, the child may even say something like, "I appreciate your decisiveness, Mother. I know in your wisdom you've made this decision for my own benefit," and thus, the "verbal" child will find a more constructive outlet for his commentary.

I'm like a kid with a new toy. I just can't wait to try this thing out. Maybe we can even return to those bucolic days of our parents' time when children were to be seen and not heard. It's almost too much to hope for.

And if we don't have to explain ourselves to our kids anymore, we'll have so much more free time. Just imagine the exhilarating feeling of liberation we'll experience. It'll be like the death of feminine foundation garments in the late '60s.

We'll have our lives back, and with them the freedom to pursue pastimes that we'd be proud to reveal on syndicated game shows and extraterrestrial beauty pageants—like advancing the cause of world peace or collecting old Avon product containers.

You gotta love those experts.

## *We Went and Spent to Vent*

LAST NIGHT I EXPERIENCED a fascinating cultural phenomenon. I subjected myself and my family to unmerciful verbal abuse and paid for the privilege. It was not unlike volunteering for an unnecessary root canal.

Actually, I didn't know exactly what I was getting into. It was pretty raw. What I was expecting was—oh, I dunno—maybe medium rare.

Welcome to a place I'll call Pete's. It's a restaurant (I think) where the waiters-slash-playground bullies sling food and insults at your table in equal portions.

Have you ever laughed at a joke you didn't get? That's what I did last night. I tittered nervously and tried not to draw attention to myself.

The menu at Pete's consists of about four things, and the waiter recites them to you like machine gun fire. Then, if you know what's good for you, you order quickly and without a trace of indecision. If you dare ask something like, "Do you have burgers?" you're likely to receive a high volume response like, "DID I *SAY* WE HAD BURGERS, MORON?"

What a fine family dining experience. Remind me to avoid it like the Ebola virus in the future.

But kids, primarily teenagers—the beasts—love this place. As soon as we entered, our eighteen year old, our darling golden boy, sprouted fangs and claws and jumped into the fray with surprising enthusiasm. In a way, it was comforting to have someone drawing all the fire from the waiters so the rest of us could stop cowering in fear. Comforting, but puzzling. This is the same kid I once read *Pat the Bunny* to.

So, of course, the psych major in me won't rest until I formulate a theory about this. That's what my bachelor's degree is good for ... sleepless nights. (Funny, I paid for that, too. I really need to reevaluate my spending habits.)

*Zo, vee need to look closely at za tendenzy of our children to indulge in aggrezzive behafiors.*

My first assessment is that none of this makes sense. Ours, after all, is a society where we teach our daughters to be assertive but encourage them to press charges of sexual harassment if someone winks at them, where we're revising history so as not to offend anyone, and where we show leniency to ax murderers because they've had troubled childhoods. Everyone is being extremely careful not to bruise the delicate sensibilities of everyone else. Yet people go to Pete's and shell out money to be berated. What's the deal?

Here goes another one of my angry junk culture explanations:

Television, radio, and movies, the fearsome threesome, bombard our kids with material that's becoming more brutal and profane by the minute. But even though a lot of the input is nasty, we expect the output to be sensitive and compassionate. Do we think our kids function as filtration systems, and garbage going in sifts through a screen and comes out sparkling and pure? If so, how do we clean their filters?

Answer: We give them opportunities to purge themselves, like going to Pete's to release all those built up toxins. That makes Pete's tantamount to a dump site for emotional human waste products, which was precisely my impression of it last night. Why kick the dog when you can go to Pete's?

So you see, our highly advanced civilization provides ingenious solutions to all our psychological needs. That's progress for you.

I think I'll pack up my family and move onto a mountain somewhere. I'd rather deal with furry predators. At least *that* food chain makes sense.

## *"Lifting" the Veil—Dangerous Business for Women*

THE OTHER DAY I WAS SITTING and having a perfectly civilized conversation with my husband and a good friend of ours, both of whom are very sensitive men and nurturing fathers, real quiche eaters. Suddenly, our friend, with a feral gleam in his eye, announced that his son had started to "lift".

First of all, let me clarify that by "lift", he didn't mean levitate. Though adolescent boys are fond of giving frequent reminders that they're full of gaseous substances, helium isn't one of them. What he's talking about is lifting weights to build muscle mass, which is something young boys are very motivated to do in light of the fact that 90% of the time they're mistaken for their mothers when they answer the phone.

Have you ever noticed that when thirteen or fourteen year old boys begin to "lift" their fathers strut about proudly as if it were an important developmental stage like getting the first tooth, taking the first step, or learning to go on the potty? What's with that?

I mean, my husband and this friend, whom I shall henceforth refer to as Rex and Thor, were getting extremely animated about this subject. Thor even bragged about going up to his son, who had complained of sore muscles after lifting, poking him in the "pecs" (a very popular word among muscle-conscious men), and asking him if it hurt there. Now, this is a man who would never dream of poking his kid in the eyes if he had a headache. It's just beyond me.

Then Rex told about how, during a particular sports season where big "pecs" are an especially desirable quality, he used to lift until he *puked* (I'm sorry—his word, not mine) and obviously, he was very proud of it. At this point I was thinking, if he'd have told me how meaningful an experience he thought that was before he proposed to me, I might have given my answer more thoughtful consideration. Here I'd always thought of puking (sorry—I won't use it again) as cause for concern, not the lure of masculine appeal.

Normally, when I find myself in a place where men begin talking about things that involve frothing at the mouth, excessive secretions, and that thing I promised not to mention again, I'm outta there pronto. But for some reason, this time I found myself paralyzed by a macabre fascination with what was happening. Before my very eyes, these two reasonable and fairly socially-presentable men were mutating into primitive life forms. This discussion was transforming them into something comparable to rutting boars. I half expected them to turn green and pop out everywhere with Incredible Hulk bulges that ripped savagely through their sleeves and pant legs. Waves of testosterone swept the room as they shared, like warriors trading battle stories, disgusting weight room tales from their vast experiences as marginally buff guys who aspire to have sons who become even buffer guys in the never-ending quest for ultimate manhood and muscular immortality.

Then I came to my senses. I began to feel the walls closing in on me. I was having trouble breathing. My vision blurred. I knew I had to escape before it was too late. Headlines: "Woman Expires from Asphyxiation due to Lethal Levels of Male Hormones."

Gasping, I made my way out of the room and to the cupboard for the antidote. I flopped on the couch, hit the remote, and breathed a sigh of relief.

Whew, that was a close one. "Steel Magnolias" wouldn't have cut it this time. I had to go for the strong stuff. As I see it, I owe *The Bridges of Madison County* my life.

## *Real Van Can Wear Pink*

IN DEFIANCE OF THE OLD stick-to-your-own-kind maxim, my minivan and I ventured onto the Chicago freeway system last week. It's a long story what we were doing there, but suffice it to say I earned my motherhood stripes for courage in the line of service to my offspring. Suffice it also to say, "You owe me, Ferdinand." (Name changed to protect the adolescent.)

Anyway, allow me to impress upon you just how out of place a polite pink and burgundy minivan feels in the company of cutthroat semi-trucks and BMWs. And until you've driven a Chicago mile in my dusty rose captain's seat, please refrain from passing judgment.

Don't act like you don't know what I'm talking about. If you've ever fought for your life on the exhaust-filled battlegrounds of a big city thoroughfare, you know just how vehicularly provincial we become when we spend our driving time on tree-lined, small town avenues and country roads.

I'm not complaining. My minivan and I love it here. Give us a deer crossing any day. We much prefer four-legged hazards to eighteen-wheeled ones. I can see clearly now, and farm equipment and Amish buggies are sights for these sore eyes. Even road kill is a thing of beauty. You just don't see any of it in the city. Apparently groundhogs, unlike me, are just too smart to go there unless they take public transportation.

I guess I'm lucky I didn't end up a bloating pink and burgundy carcass on the roadside. I could see early on nobody was going to make allowances for the country cousin. One either had to be a semi or a compact—a bully or a mosquito—barging or flitting. My minivan has been trained in neither barging nor flitting techniques. It only knows how to amble, and ambling doesn't cut it in the big leagues.

I felt as if I had walked into a boardroom meeting with a diaper bag instead of an attache case.

In an area of dense population, my van screams bumpkin. Heck, my van screams bumpkin here at home, but at least here its sleeker minivan neighbors are somewhat accepting. In Chicago, they tried to make me eat their dust.

The operative word there is "tried." We corn-fed country minivan operators will only eat so much dust before we get our hackles up and start dishing out a little dust of our own. Then it becomes survival of the fittest.

So with my dear Ferdinand looking on, ol' Mom offered up a little lesson in the remarkable ability of our species, the rural driver, to adapt to challenging environmental conditions.

I barged, flitted, sped up, dodged, cut off, and, by golly, got me and mine where we wanted to go. And though my child grinned and teasingly accused me of "stooping to their level," I saw the pride in his eyes. I think Mom's fighting instinct surprised him a little, and he saw that although I had to get tough, I didn't allow myself to engage in any truly low-life behaviors like obscene gesturing or, a current favorite, ear-biting.

So, like I said, we got there. Then we had to face another big city challenge: parking. I'm prepared to swear in court that those parking lot attendants are in constant communication with each other and run a highly sophisticated scam on customers from rural areas.

They saw me coming. The sign said six dollars but the attendant charged me eight and when I tried to protest, pretended he couldn't speak English. I'm guessing he had a lookout posted to alert him to oncoming suckers.

In impeccable English, the tip probably came in via radio and went something like this:

"Personnel in Lot 382 please be advised of approaching rube in pink and burgundy minivan. Driver appears traumatized and receptive to posted parking rate bait-and-switch maneuver. Activate language non-fluency strategy ASAP."

At that point, the fight went out of me, and I paid the extra two bucks. Hadn't I already slain the freeway dragons? Why be greedy? Next trip I could take on big city parking corruption. I knew I was van enough to do it.

After all, I am strong. I am invincible. I am minivan.

## *Odiferous and Sensuous—Scents-R-Us*

Perhaps you should give more thought to how you smell. Think about it—fragrance is a form of self-definition. You might drive a Lexus, wear designer suits, and carry an attache case of cordovan leather, but if you still smell like Tinkerbell you might not be commanding the respect you deserve from the guys in the boardroom.

Let's look at the recent history of fragrance. (Recent, because I don't feel like doing any research.) In the sixties, when men were men and women were women and any variation on that was just one of them darn hippies, guys wore *Brute* and girls wore *Chantilly*. Them hippie-types wore Patchouli, and everyone knew where they stood. Life was simple.

But as the years passed and individuality was invented, new fragrances were developed that enabled each person to express his or her own unique taste and characteristics. Like *CK-One*, the scent for men *or* women (or dogs or guppies or whatever). So you see, individuality is the key to fragrance selection.

And the names of perfumes are significant, too. Take *Chanel*, for example. It connotes elegance and affluence. *Eternity* implies that the fragrance is so memorable it lives on into infinity. This is signified by the TV ads in which two people are necking on a beach and remain lip-locked while waves crash over them, sucking them into the undertow. These people are so in love because of the way she smells that they don't even stop sucking face to save themselves. Now *that's* romantic.

Then there are the black and white *Obsession* ads, which feature a man lusting after a woman who is obsessed with scrubbing everything in sight: the floor, the stairs, the furniture. I'd call this one *Retention*, but I'm not a market wizard.

How about the commercial with the line-up of adolescents that look like malnourished refugees who haven't bathed in months? Apparently, they use that particular perfume to cover the smell.

Frankly, I find it refreshing that there's a movement toward honest, natural names for fragrances—like *Grass*, *Rain*, *Green Apple*, etc. Of course, that doesn't explain names like *Sunflower*, a cologne whose namesake has no scent, but some mysteries of the world of concocted smells will forever baffle. And speaking of mysterious names, what's up with some of the foreign-sounding ones—like *Jontue*? What's is *that*? Sure it has a nice sound, but for all we know it means something like "fungus" in French.

"Pierre, it appears you have an acute case of jontue between your toes."

It's frightening what blind faith we place in the hands of merchants.

Backing up a bit, I've got to tell you about a friend of mine who wears the scent called *Grass*. This is proof positive how authentic this cologne is:

He tells me he was walking in downtown Chicago recently, wearing *Grass*. Presumably he was wearing clothes, too, but with this particular friend you never really know. Anyway, in Chicago, as in any other big city, you have to look long and hard to find a blade of grass, so my friend was smelling especially fresh and natural at the time. This was confirmed when he walked past one of those horse-drawn carriages you occasionally see transporting highly artificially perfumed patrons to dinner or the theater.

What happened then was that the horse stopped, lifted his head, and flaring his nostrils, looked lustfully at my friend. For one heart-stopping moment, he thought maybe the animal would charge him, knock him down and start to graze. All men his age fear hair loss, so you can imagine his anxiety. Thank heaven, the beast mastered his primitive urges, as any sophisticated Chicago horse would, and my friend passed unharmed.

Let this be a lesson to you outdoorsy types who wear musk colognes. Stay out of the woods during deer mating season. Ol' Bambi isn't as innocent as he would have you believe.

Despite these inherent risks, I like the idea of fragrances that are real and natural. As another option, I also like the idea of fragrances that are tailored to our lifestyles. So I've come up with a few ideas for signature scents for people with specific interests and occupations. Read on.

How about one for stay-at-home moms with small children? It could be called *Formulique*, *Eau de Graham Crackers*, or *Barney Balm*. One for business executives called *VIP-One*, *Parfum de Plutocrat*, or *Entrepreneuria*. For a doctor: *Comaroma*, *Hippocra-tease*, or *Surgical Spice*. For a policeman: *Law and Odor*. A golfer: *Bogey Bouquet* or *Le Whiff*. A dentist: *Implacable* or *Impressions*. Alternative musician: *Rock Reek*. Minister: *Blessed Essence*. My husband's favorite for a veterinarian: *L'air du Tomcat*. And for your basic white, Anglo-Saxon protestant: *Wisp of Wasp*.

I have more, but without copyright protection, I'm understandably reluctant to reveal them. But you get the drift, or shall I say, the waft.

Anyway, give a little thought to your smell. And remember, if you wear *Grass* into inner-city areas, carry sugar cubes for protection. And no wearing *Green Apple* around worms.

# *Passages: Worry a Little, Whine a Little, Then Suck It Up and Move On*

## *An Easy Delivery* (*re:* My First Column)

ALRIGHT, DEEP CLEANSING BREATH. Get a grip, girl. This isn't childbirth. It's a column, not a baby, and the only contractions going on around here are the kind you learned in English class.

Still, I can't help but notice the similarities. I'm definitely in the transition phase of labor, no doubt about that. The big difference is I'm not feeling an urge to push or to grab some forceps and use them to remove my husband's liver. The element of aggression appears to be missing. Also, I have a tremendous feeling of anticipation, but it's a how's-it-gonna-turn-out instead of a will-it-be-a-boy-or-girl kind of anticipation. And while we're on the subject, let me assure you there will be no gender bias here. I refuse to stoop to the kind of senseless male-bashing that's currently so popular. Trust me. I will speak in a universally sensitive language that everyone can understand—even men.

Really, I like men. I married one.

But I digress. The deal is, every week I'm going to give birth to a new column. And every week I will endeavor to approach the birth process with renewed excitement in the knowledge that I won't have to sit on a donut cushion afterward.

Then each week after I've borne my creation, I'll bask in the euphoria of giving life to something enduring, something that will make its mark in the annals of mankind... without the painful swelling of tissues.

Don't get me wrong, I don't mean to minimize the magic and wonder of the childbirth experience. It's really dandy. I've done it three magically, wonderful times. It's just that I can see some real advantages to birthing a column over birthing a baby. After all, I doubt if I'll ever push hard enough on the keyboard to break blood vessels in my eyes or develop ugly purple marks from stretching my imagination. And with any luck I won't need stitches from opening my mind to new ideas.

Just as having my babies was the fulfillment of a dream so, too, is this column. It all started when my dear sister-in-law shared with me something that had always held great meaning for her. And it was simply this: A closed mouth gathers no foot. Then my mother said something very prophetic: If you keep crossing your eyes like that, they'll stick that way. But that wasn't the really important thing I was referring to.

She said to me, "Marilyn, if you don't straighten up no one will ever take you seriously."

And then it occurred to me, like a beacon through the darkness. This is my destiny. To prattle on in a senseless and ludicrous manner and *get paid to do it*!

Life is good.

So here I am, perched on the edge of the great delivery table of life, feet planted stalwartly in the stirrups of fate, poised for my leap into columnisthood. Pass out the cigars.

## *Braving the Birds and the Bees*

THE FOLLOWING COLUMN IS ABOUT THE FACTS OF LIFE. Aha! I hear pages rattling all over town—you're all snapping to attention. Pretty cheap ploy to increase my readership, huh?

But seriously folks, telling your children the facts of life is a little like playing a game of touch football. It seems like it would be easy enough, but you end up being bumped, jostled, tripped up, knocked down, faked out, and evaded, so that once you cross the goal line, you're not really sure whether you were playing offense or defense or even if you're in the right end zone ...

Did you follow that? Because, frankly, you have the same look on your face my kids did when I told them about the birds and the bees cross-pollinating and laying eggs.

Let me start at the beginning. And I'll warn you, I'm not going to use names because when it comes to my kids' humiliation index, this subject is the Big Kahuna.

I've always heard that the experts say the best way to impart information about sex to children is to answer the questions as they come, simply and honestly, and only to elaborate as needed, according to the child's degree of interest.

Horse spittle.

Are the experts *crazy*? Let me just say this: I have a seventeen year old who never *did* ask, and I'm darn sure he's interested. It's not like he comes home every day and tells me about what he learned at school. At his age, he paws the ground once for yes and twice for no. Verbal communication with Mom is not a priority. How likely is he now, or has he ever been, to pull me aside and say, "Mother, would you have a few moments to clear up some confusion I have about reproduction?"

So much for having a plan. I recommend force-feeding kids the information. Otherwise, you'll end up with a pretty old kid who thinks your dog has to marry the neighbor's dog in order to produce puppies, an issue that came up at our house. Pretty embarrassing when the child's father is a veterinarian, even though it did exhibit a comfortingly traditional moral standard.

One technique we resorted to was the captive audience approach. My husband took one of the kids on a camping trip and ever so casually brought up the subject. Now I don't care how smooth you are, the kid will always look like a deer caught in your headlights. Evidently my husband did all the talking and when he asked if there were any questions, this particular child said, "Yes. I have a horrible headache. Can we go to sleep now?" followed by a long pause and, "That's really gross, Dad."

How insightful that he'd utilize the time-honored headache excuse. But at least the kid had the facts, distasteful as they were.

I tried the academic approach with another of the kids. I got a straight-shooting, illustrated book and sat down with my child to engage in a mature discussion. We opened to the first chapter which dealt with entry-level info about male and female physiology. You would've thought the pictures were of Jim Carrey and Roseanne Barr. The kid started to titter. It grew to guffaws and then to side-splitting, tear-rolling hysteria. I cashed in my chips for the evening.

But I got her back. On a forty-five minute drive to the mall a week later, I delivered the pertinent information machine-gun style. She never knew what hit her.

The point is that this is something that will never be easy for parents *or* kids. Face it, they don't want to hear it and you don't want to say it. But you have to, otherwise they'll go on a fact-finding mission on the playground someday and hear that gestation is 23 months long and conception occurs when the moon is in the seventh house and Jupiter aligns with Mars. Consider it one of life's major challenges that, once conquered, gives you a great sense of accomplishment.

Me? Mission mercifully accomplished. Now I'm going to climb Mt. Everest.

## *Kissing Boo-Boos Pooh-Poohed as No-No for Mama*

I REMEMBER WHEN THE SLIGHTEST STUB of a toe sent my kids into hysterics. Heck, I remember that a couple of them would cry when a trip didn't even turn into a full-fledged fall. Just the idea of what could've happened was terribly traumatic for them.

I'm not saying they were babies (even though they actually *were* at the time), I'm just saying they liked their boo-boos acknowledged. They also liked them kissed and covered with super-hero bandages. Bandages were miracle cures back then. Life was much simpler.

Now that my kids are older, all that has changed. Most of their boo-boos occur on a playing field, and not only am I not supposed to run out and kiss them, I'm not even allowed to let my metabolic rate become elevated. I have to will myself to be serene. I'm thinking about taking up yoga to help with this.

Yep, I'm learning to squelch my impulses and control my outward behavior, even if I feel like little bolts of motherly instinct are attacking me like burrowing chiggers. Once I've mastered this, I'll be ready to take on Navy Seal training.

I have to keep reminding myself that kids are tough. Their bodies can get hit, fly across the field, crash, and bounce back for more, as if they have springs strapped on their backsides. If I got hit like that, I'd wind up on life-support.

My daughter was tripped in a game recently and flipped over like a malfunctioning pinwheel, arms and legs everywhere. I couldn't believe she got back up. I also couldn't believe she didn't wrap her lacrosse stick around her opponent's neck. (I'd need yoga for that, too.) I stayed fairly calm that time because she rolled right to her feet.

But another time, I needed some coaching. My son was hit in the knee by a ball during a little league game. Far better than the reverse of that, but frightening nonetheless. When it occurred, I had time to do no more than stiffen my posture before my husband was issuing urgent instructions under his breath …

"Don't get—don't get up—don't get up! Stay calm—he'll be okay—See, he's getting up—now take a deep breath—easy."

Easy for him to say. He was a macho-studnik ball player himself once. If I ever pulled a muscle cheerleading, I made a big, fat, teeth-gritting deal out of it.

A friend of mine tells me it doesn't pay to react too quickly when your kid's injured. Her son got knocked down playing junior high soccer once and stayed on the ground for what seemed like an interminable period of time to her. She remembered how he had instructed her not to do anything to embarrass him if he ever got hurt on the field. Apparently the injury itself would have been much less painful than being regarded as a mama's boy. So she stayed put until she couldn't stand it any longer, but as she started to get up, he jumped to his feet and resumed playing. Later she asked him where he was hurt, and he explained to her that the team was short on players and there were no substitutes. The coach had told them if they got knocked down, to stay down as long as possible so everyone could get a rest. I believe "milk it" were his words.

I knew it was not a case of catching a breather when my daughter went down again during a lacrosse game the other day. I had a perfect view as about five lacrosse sticks came down on what appeared to be the bridge of her nose. Of course, they wear no face protection except for a mouth guard. I'd be a lot happier if they wore Hannibal Lecter masks, but there's no chance of that. I asked.

Anyway, she landed face down on the ground as a little voice that sounded like a chipmunk version of my husband's told me, "Don't get up—stay calm—take a deep breath!" Meanwhile, my womb contracted and my eyeballs broke into a sweat. I kept seeing the replay in my head as she lay on the ground. I was sure she'd look like someone from the Maraschino Brothers' Collection Agency when she got up—her nose pointing toward her left ear or similarly asymmetrical.

I couldn't see any blood. That was good. She was staying down. That was bad. The officials weren't screaming and fainting. That was good. They did, however, look grave. That was bad.

Finally, she struggled to her feet and was helped to the sidelines. Praises be, her face was just the way I'd left it, in its original genetic design. Whew! So much for the Cruella de Vil, cool and unconcerned routine. I was over to the sidelines like a supersonic minivan. Her chin was swollen and her jaw sore, but nothing was missing or relocated, so I chucked her on the shoulder with a cocky "Attagirl" and sauntered back to my seat. No big deal. Just another little, inconsequential bump in the life of a veteran athlete's mom.

But you can bet your stadium cushion, once she was in the privacy of home with the door closed behind her, that nasty ol' boo-boo got a kiss from Mom. Sure made *me* feel better.

## *Animal, Vegetable, Mineral, or Chemical? A Hairy Decision*

I NEED A CHANGE. I need to jog my life out of the complacent little routine it's fallen into. I need, figuratively, to scale the highest mountain and swim the deepest sea. To spread my wings and soar to the pinnacle of self evaluation, to look down deep into my soul, and challenge myself to actualize—to make brave and brilliant changes in what is fundamentally me.

I think I'll get a perm.

Oh, I know it sounds like a daring, even reckless, life changing decision. But it's one I'm prepared to make in the name of personal growth.

And it's a quick fix.

After all, what woman hasn't at one time or another thought that maybe it will be this particular hairstyle, this time, that will transform her into an ethereally beautiful creature of such poise and stature that she can face the world fearlessly and quote those immortal words, (written by the great philosophers of the Pantene Shampoo advertising department and rehearsed to perfection for months on end by a vacant-eyed but ethereally beautiful spokeswoman), "Don't hate me because I'm beautiful."

(I think there was supposed to be a question mark somewhere in that sentence.)

Anyway, it's worth the gamble, and drastic changes in my hairstyle don't scare me. When I was a kid, my mother broke me in hard. She had this saying that she used when my hair got a little out of control, "Marilyn, you look like a sheep peeping out of a brush heap."

Once she decided to have my long hair cut into the popular "Pixie" style of the time. I went from Little Lord Fauntleroy to Peter Pan in one fell swoop of the scissors. Then a year or so later, it was the fashionable, sleek-crowned look with the tightly-permed coil of curls just below the earlobes. Over time, I came out from under the bed and learned to adapt. In junior high and high school, I swept through the big leagues: Diana Ross, Cher, and Farrah Fawcett.

As a matter of fact, we're all pretty hair-hardened in my family. Over the years, I've taught my husband and kids to be adaptable, too.

When we were dating, Jim asked me to cut his hair—and to this day I'd swear to it in court—very short, especially on top. The fact that his buddies called him names like Obleo and Conehead for the next several weeks was not my fault.

Then there was the time I cut my son's hair right before school pictures, and he asked me to give it the bilevel, sort of wedged look the boys were all wearing. Fortunately, we have the school yearbook to commemorate the unique, shingled A-frame effect I created for him.

And another time was when my daughter ended up with about a half inch fringe of bangs after I tried to cut them outside on the patio. The wind was blowing and I had to keep evening them up.

Now my brave offspring are taking this hard-won coiffure courage into their own arenas.

In the final week of the season for the high school swim team just prior to the big district meet, my son and his teammates count down the days with a different hair event each day. First they bleach it. Then they dye sections of it colors like lime, mango, and bubble gum. Then they shave patterns in it and mousse it into imaginative sculptures. Finally on the day before districts, just as they're beginning to look a little Rodman-esque, they shave it all off so as to reduce drag in the water (pardon the pun).

My daughter commented that it would be fun to be able to do that. To do absolutely anything you wanted to your hair because you knew you were going to shave it all off eventually. She assuaged her longing by putting a plum-colored rinse on her hair for one of her lacrosse games. It washed out, thank heaven. I don't think I could've dealt with two shaved heads in the family. I don't care if Demi did it.

My niece lives in Minneapolis, the hair capital of the free world. She says there's more hair per capita there than in any other U.S. city. Lots of sheep peeping out of brush heaps. I went to visit. She's right. I saw every imaginable color of dreadlock and spike sported by intriguingly androgynous individuals. (And there wasn't a swimming pool in sight.) There were also lots of what I call UFOs, unidentifiable frizzed overhangs. Plus many other amazing dos. It's the Minneapolis version of "big hair". I don't think it's any coincidence that the world's biggest mall is there, too.

What is it about self expression and hair? Don't people write poetry anymore?

Anyway, I'm going to take the leap and make the midlife change to chemically-induced self actualization.

I'll try not to think about my friend whose husband and kids called her broccolihead after she got her perm.

On the other hand ... maybe I'll tell my hairdresser just to trim a little off the ends.

## *Mall-Adjusted Children*

WHEN IT COMES TO FASHION FORECASTING, the mall is the Nostradamus of our time. I'm almost afraid to go there anymore. I don't know if it's because it always makes me feel like the Queen of Frump or because I'm afraid of its influence on my kids.

For example, there are more body pierces per capita at the mall than at any other place known to modern man. The typical clerk resembles a pie safe. I saw one the last time I was there who could've strained spaghetti through his ear.

And it's very distracting being waited on by someone with a pierced tongue. I find myself wishing he (or she) would get a rhythm going and synchronize his oral percussion with his speech pattern. It sounds like a Fred Astaire tap routine gone awry on his molars.

Here's a curiosity: How do they affix the backs on those studs they wear in their noses? With the cost of the piercing, they must include a surgical instrument that enables them to reach far up into the unnavigated region between the frontal lobes of their brains and their sinuses.

A while back my daughter, under the influence of mall exposure, talked me into letting her get a second set of pierces in her earlobes. I'm still traumatized. I can't shake the remorse I feel about authorizing this senseless mutilation, but her last protracted, grating "PLEEEEZ?!" was like fingernails on a blackboard. It shattered my resolve.

I used arguments that evidently meant nothing to her.

I told her I gestated very sincerely over those earlobes for a full nine months. I cut out caffeine and artificial sweeteners, took prenatal vitamins, and thought positive thoughts, and I *didn't* do it so she'd have a nice smooth surface to poke holes in at random.

I told her it all seemed innocent right now, but before she knew it one hole would lead to another. Then the desire for more pierces would spin crazily out of control, and she wouldn't be able to stop until she looked like nylon net. Of course, there'd be many handy uses for her around the house, but she'd be a mere shadow of her former self.

Then I played my trump card: Infection. This is a girl for whom pain has always been a great deterrent. A tiny splinter can provoke cataclysmic hysteria. The sight of a sweat bee can send her into orbit. I decided to tread gingerly so as not to overplay my hand.

"You'll get gangrene and your ears will turn black and putrid and fall off," I blurted out.

She looked at me blankly for a full minute. I couldn't read her thoughts clearly but I think they fell somewhere between, "This does not compute" and "If I dignify that with a response all hope for reason will be lost."

The silence stretched between us like a wasteland, and in it I felt the inevitable: The time had come to relinquish control, to place a tiny notch in a single apron string, to grant her sovereignty over her own earlobes.

Then it came.

"PLEEEZ?!"

The final lunge for which I had no parry. I knew I was defeated.

So now I've retreated to more defensible ground. I'm just glad there's no tattoo parlor at the mall.

## *Campus Scenery: Babes vs. Plaster Cows*

I'VE ACCOMPANIED A COUPLE OF MY YOUNG ASSOCIATES, whose identities I shall endeavor to protect, on several college visits this summer. Finding a school that's just the "right fit" for these two kids has been a fascinating, albeit challenging, process.

I don't remember it being so complicated when I was their age, but then I'm a simple gal with simple tastes. There was a pretty good school down the road a piece, so I went there. Then, when I got tired of it, I transferred to another one a little farther down the road, and it was just fine. Of course, I didn't have aspirations to be a genetic engineer or a nuclear physicist. In fact, I still don't know what I want to be when I grow up. I just knew I wanted to broaden my scope, which I ultimately did. I am, indeed, much broader now than I was then, but I'm not certain how much a higher education had to do with that.

Now, for the sake of discussion, let's just say one of the kids I've been going on college visits with is my own son. And so as not to confuse him with any person living or dead, let's give him a fictitious name like, say, Ferdinand.

So here's the deal. Ferdinand and I picked out three schools to visit based on very important criteria: The first college because it's very strong in his prospective major. The second because of it's outstanding reputation as a liberal arts institution. And the third, because a major men's magazine ranked it number one in the nation for good looking girls. So you can see we were very cautious not to limit our perspective too severely.

We hit the ground running, and in a two-day period managed to see three very different colleges.

On day one, I found out what my more experienced friends meant when they told me the kid has to get the right "feel" for a school from the very beginning. As we were preparing to turn into the entrance of the first college, we passed a building that had a fifteen-foot plaster cow on it's roof. At this juncture, Ferdinand began to emit a very negative guttural sound that left little doubt that this particular bastion of education had offended his aesthetic sensibilities. And as we went through the motions of taking a tour of the campus, nary a brown blade of grass escaped his notice. Moo U. was blackballed.

At the next two colleges, we made it past the front gates unoffended and embarked on our tours. The parents in the group asked all the usual questions concerning things like dorm security, books and fees, and work-study opportunities, while the kids grilled the tour guides on issues of critical kid importance like whether the local pizza place delivers to the dorms and if a major is offered in ultimate frisbee.

I picked up from the general tone of the group that most of the kids were a bit fuzzy yet about what their majors would be. But, as in any college tour group, there was the occasional outstanding kid who knew with complete certainty that he or she would major in something like pre-geriatric cardiopulmonary marine management.

Just a word here to those of you who are new at this. I have learned that kids like this are the pod-children of extraterrestrial aliens. Do not feel threatened by their supreme confidence. In fact, if you can arrange for your child to room with one of them, it can be a real advantage. They set a marvelous example with their superior study skills and lack of interest in social interaction. Plus, it provides your child an exotic place to visit during holiday breaks.

If you're really lucky during a tour of the residence halls, you might get to meet an R.A. This is traditionally a very wholesome looking older student with a dazzling smile whose job it is to be sure your child adheres to all dorm policies such as flossing daily and eating plenty of dark green leafy vegetables.

When our college tours were all over and it was time to meet with admissions counselors, I was ready to get to the bottom line. While all the talk of fine academic traditions was well and good, I had my own acid test. This was the question I asked:

"What kind of guarantee can you give me that if I sink half my life's savings into your institution, my little Ferdie will meet the woman of his dreams, graduate and earn a six-figure income, give me a slew of adorable grandchildren, and call home frequently to express his undying affection to the people who gave him life?"

And do you know, those guys—educated as they are—never had a ready answer for me?

So I guess the final decision will go back to what kind of feel my child has for the place.

Right now, he's leaning toward the school with the number one babe ranking.

## *Graduation Traumatization*

TWENTY-FOUR MORE DAYS and it's one down and two to go. Then it's party time for the hubby and me.

No kidding—I'm just peachy about my first-born's graduation from high school. It signals the beginning of a new era for us. In a few short years, Jim and I will be wearing gold chains and jet-setting around the world, unencumbered by pesky kids. We'll be shaking castanets in Madrid and the snow off our ski boots in the Alps (not to mention our booties on dance floors in all the "places to be seen" around the globe).

That's right, we are pushing that first little chickie out of the nest with an enthusiastic flurry of the feathers of future freedom. No sloppy sentiment here. No sir. (sniff) …

SWEET MERCIFUL LORD, I'M BEGGING YOU TO GET MY BLUBBERING SOUL THROUGH THIS WITH AT LEAST A MICROSCOPIC SHRED OF DIGNITY.

… a moment, please, to compose myself—

Okay, so maybe I'm not quite as *in control* as I would have you believe. So maybe I *am* spending long, desperate hours rocking in a corner clutching one of his Cookie Monster slippers to my chest and staring vacantly into space. I'm a survivor. You'll see. I'll be just fine. They'll just up the dosage of my medication a bit.

How is the hubby taking it? Well, he naturally feels somewhat the same, but he's got the male take on the issue. His feelings are compounded by concern about next fall's substantial drop in liquid assets. In his case, it's not only the anticipation of the boy's secession from the union, so to speak, but the upcoming hardship of The Great Depression. Men do tend to worry unnaturally about peripheral details like food on the table.

I, on the other hand, am concerned about important things like how all this effects my mood. I assure you, I'm not totally dysfunctional twenty-four/seven. At least thirty minutes a day, I recognize this is all part of the master plan. We're loaned these cute little dimpled bundles with the understanding that we'll feed 'em, love 'em, and guide 'em for a finite period of time and then set them free to make their contribution to mankind. It really stinks, if you ask me.

I don't know why we just can't keep them. This isn't pilot dog fostering. I never signed a official agreement to relinquish custody at the end of an eighteen-year training period. Where do I go to appeal?

I don't mean to be a troublemaker, but where's the fairness in all this? I had to sit up all night long through bouts of croup, help with math homework that would deaden the brain cells of a CPA, and fend off adolescent attitude attacks that made python wrestling an appealing alternative. And now, just when he's getting to be a really cool human with the minimum of upkeep, I have to release him into the wild? What a raw deal. I've been ripped off before, but this one takes the cake.

I guess the question *now* is: Can I battle my way back from this cruel stroke of fate only to have to do it all over again two more times in the next five years? (Factor in that I'm a big baby.)

Personally, I don't know the answer. I guess I'll just have to get back to you on that one.

## *Mom's First Prom*

FORGIVE ME IF I SOUND A BIT MAUDLIN TODAY. My views are colored by sleep deprivation. I was up all night last weekend, and I'm like a baby thrown off schedule. But at the same time, I feel as old as the hills.

I've just lived through my first prom as a parent. And to enhance the sentimentality inherent in the experience, I chaperoned the post-prom party. This involved the all-nighter, which is something I never did even in college. That just proves what kind of twisted influence parenthood can have on a formerly sensible person.

I have a theory. I'm convinced that high school proms are part of a master plan to ease the fledgling from the nest causing as little separation anxiety to the parents as possible. While we're busy admiring our prom-polished offspring—flesh of our flesh—taking credit for these marvelous creations of ours, life's quiet current is moving us downstream away from them ever so subtly.

As I looked at the elegant girls and handsome boys on prom night (I can't bring myself to use "men/women" terminology yet), I could hardly believe these were the same kids I'd watched, all sweaty and exuberant, on sports fields and at school functions over the past several years. Were these the same boys who had sacked out on my living room floor dozens of times, awakening sleepy-eyed and groggy with their hair sticking out in every direction? Couldn't be.

But apparently this growing up thing is going to happen. Our little craft is going to make its way downstream no matter how we paddle against the current. One minute you're tying a tiny tennis shoe, and the next you're adjusting a bow tie and smoothing the lapels of a tuxedo. It's then that you realize, as you step back to admire your handiwork, that it's beginning to acquire the look of a finished product. It's a real jolt.

Then I saw his date. And if there was the tiniest remnant of denial left in me that these dear ones were becoming young adults, she was the vision that put it to rest.

Thank heaven for the post-prom party, where the gilt coach turned back into a pumpkin and the kids turned back into that bumping, jostling litter of puppies I recognized. I heaved a sigh of relief as I realized they were still kids, after all, and the earlier images were a mere glimpse through the window of things to come, still somewhat threatening but at least not something I had to cope with all at once.

Then as I turned to survey the scene, something caught my eye. It was a big kid who was showing so much enthusiasm for the game he was playing, he stood out in the crowd. It was my husband. He was also there in the official capacity of chaperone, but this confirmed my suspicion that he knew better than to miss a good party. Suddenly I felt a bit of the pup myself.

And it came to me. Maybe that glimpse through the window of things to come doesn't have to look so dismal after all … as long as we remember to leave a door open.